GIRL RISING

CHANGING THE WORLD ONE GIRL AT A TIME

TANYA LEE STONE

in association with GIRLRISING

WENDY
LAMB
BOOKS

Library of Congress Cataloging-in-Publication Data
Names: Stone, Tanya Lee, author.
Title: Girl rising : changing the world one girl at a time / by Tanya Lee Stone.
Description: First edition. | New York : Wendy Lamb Books, an imprint of Random House Childrens
Books, a division of Penguin Random House LLC, [2017] | Audience: Age 12–up. — | Audience: Grade 9
to 12. — | Includes bibliographical references and index.
Identifiers: LCCN 2015026152 | ISBN 978-0-553-51146-8 (trade : alk. paper) | ISBN 978-0-553-51147-5
(lib. bdg. : alk. paper) | ISBN 978-0-553-51148-2 (ebook) | ISBN 978-0-553-51149-9 (pbk. : alk. paper)
Subjects: LCSH: Girls—Education—Cross-cultural studies—Juvenile literature. | Girls—Conduct of life—
Juvenile literature. | Social change—Juvenile literature.
Classification: LCC LC1707 .S86 2016 | DDC 371.822—dc23

The text of this book is set in 11.7-point Adobe Garamond Pro.

MANUFACTURED IN CHINA
10 9 8 7 6 5 4 3 2 1
First Edition

For all the girls who fight for what is not given them,
and for all the people who help them.   —T.L.S.

Schoolgirls, Nepal.

CONTENTS

Girl Rising film crew, Peru.

WHY (AND HOW) A FILM BECAME A BOOK

In April 2013 I saw the film *Girl Rising,* in which we meet nine powerful girls and hear their inspiring stories. These girls escaped situations that keep millions of girls worldwide from getting an education. Theirs are stories of hope that represent what is possible but not yet happening on a large-enough scale.

The day after I saw the film, the girls were still very much with me. Their words, their tears, their triumphs were seared into my soul. I had a growing sense of the enormity of the topic—and of how little I really knew. What *are* the major obstacles to education, and what causes them in the first place? Why are these issues so much more of a problem for girls than for boys? What can we do about what seems to be an overwhelming global problem?

As there is only so much content any film can tackle in ninety minutes, my "book brain" kicked into high gear. How many other girls did the filmmakers interview to be able to narrow it down to nine? Did they have footage of all those girls? Photographs?

I started thinking about how to expand the material so people could learn even more. To my mind, that meant explaining each obstacle to education, while adding stories from many other girls to show how widespread these problems are.

Luckily for me, the *Girl Rising* producers were excited about my idea and embraced it. They shared more than forty-five hours of raw video interview footage from all the girls they met via organizations running successful girl-focused programs in the countries they visited. They also shared the field notes from the director, Richard Robbins, and the producers. With these astounding resources, combined with my own research, I began a journey to create a nonfiction narrative informed and inspired by their film. The product of that journey is this book; the process has been life-changing.

Tanya Lee Stone

PART ONE

THE STAKES

"When you get an education, you become part of society. Without an education, you are left out."

—PRIYA, INDIA

"Life without an education is like a book with blank pieces of paper."

—PURNIMA, NEPAL

"My life would mean very little without school."

—DOUAA, EGYPT

It is easy to notice only our own place in the world—what's right in front of us, and around us, and has been since the second we became conscious beings. When we are babies, our limited view of the world focuses on the people in our immediate family. Soon we notice our home, our neighborhood, our town. As we grow, we begin to see a wider picture of the world and the people with whom we share it. After all, there are more than seven billion other people on earth.

What happens to all those other people affects what happens to us, whether or not we know it, or choose to pay attention. Money, war, natural disasters, literacy, education—these are all factors that have wide-sweeping influences that connect us to each other, whether we live in a small town in Iowa or a village in Sierra Leone or a city in Thailand. What happens to our fellow citizens on earth shapes all of us.

This may sound simple, but it's an important place to start when we think about the ways in which the world could change to make it a more balanced, more humane, more functional place. When it comes to education, one fact affects us all: world-wide, over 62 million girls* are not in school. Why is this, and why is it so important?

* While the majority of data points to 62 million, these numbers are extremely difficult to measure, and in 2016, UNESCO reported that the number may be as high as 130 million.

"I want to stand for children who are suffering like I did."

—FANTA, SIERRA LEONE

"THERE ARE A MILLION YOUNG MALALAS"

By now, you have probably heard the story of Malala Yousafzai, who spoke out publicly against the Taliban (a fundamentalist Islamic group) for destroying girls' schools in her native Pakistan. She was just ten years old. The following year, she wrote blog posts for the British Broadcasting Corporation (BBC) about girls' right to education. At first, she used a fake name because it was dangerous to speak out publicly. But even after her identity was revealed, she continued her work and was acknowledged for it, winning Pakistan's National Youth Peace Prize in 2011.

Her bold actions put her life at risk. In October 2012, when she was fifteen, a young Taliban man boarded her school bus and shot her point-blank in the head. Somehow Malala survived that gunshot. She continued to speak out, undaunted. In 2014, Malala became the youngest person to win a Nobel Peace Prize.

As phenomenal as Malala is, she would likely be the first to agree that she is not alone on her mission. Around the globe, girls are fighting for a better life: escaping forced labor, refusing to be married too young, sacrificing their safety to change long-held traditions. They are fighting to become educated and make the world a better place in the process. As former British prime minister Gordon Brown wrote, "There are a million young Malalas."

You may think you have nothing in common with many of these girls—that they lead lives that are completely different from yours, that they are "other" kinds of girls who live in "other" kinds of places. That is not true.

Girls are girls, no matter where they live. These are girls with sisters, brothers, cousins, aunts, uncles, mothers, fathers. Girls with best friends, sharing secrets. Girls playing their favorite music, swimming, jumping, playing, dreaming, working.

One thing about their lives is dramatically different, though: the opportunity to go to school and get an education is not something they can count on. It is something they must fight for.

Most young people in developed nations (nations with a high level of industry and standard of living—for example, Great Britain, America, and most of Europe)—get up in the morning and head to school without a second thought, because free public education is available to all. But in more than fifty countries, school is not free, and often, students and their families cannot pay.

We look at numbers and facts all the time without necessarily understanding how significant they are. But this number—the 62 million girls who are not in school—profoundly affects how our whole world functions.

Why? Because educating girls literally changes how nations behave. Educating girls changes how governments function. It changes economies and jobs. It changes the shape of health care. It changes how families are raised. It can change entire cultures.

"I want to share my life with you. Where should I start?"
—Rosematrie, Haiti

THE RIPPLE EFFECT

How can sending a girl to school do all these things? Fifty percent of the world's population is female. If half of the seven billion people on the planet were educated, and thus able to be employed and more likely to be in better health, they would make the world better for all of us. Many leaders understand this. In January 2015, India's prime minister, Narendra Modi, launched his Beti Bachao Beti Padhao (Save the Daughter, Teach the Daughter) campaign. On a visit to India a few days later, U.S. president Barack Obama said, "When a girl goes to school, it doesn't just open up her young mind, it benefits all of us. . . . Maybe someday she'll start her own business, or invent a new technology or cure a disease. And when women are able to work, families are healthier, communities are wealthier, and entire countries are more prosperous. . . . If nations really want to succeed in today's global economy, they can't simply ignore the talents of half their people."

When you invest in a girl, it affects not only her, but also her children, and her children's children. Let's call this the ripple effect. When household income is in the hands of a woman, she is far more likely to invest in her family and local community than a man is. This significantly boosts the economy and the overall health of a nation.

The stories you will read here are about girls who have been able to escape their circumstances and go to school. Their stories represent hope for the potential of millions of others. The stakes are high. There are many risk factors that can doom a girl to a life of poverty and struggle. Education is the key to skipping over those pitfalls.

The act of educating girls is the single most powerful tool we have to make the world a safer, healthier, more functional place.

... she is likely to marry and have children later.

FACT

A girl who receives 7 years of education marries 4 years later and has 2.2 fewer children.[1]

... there will be fewer infant deaths.

FACT

The baby of a mother under 18 has a 60% greater risk of dying before his or her first birthday than the baby of a mother over 19.[2]

When you EDUCATE a girl...

... she will be able to get a better job.

FACT

An extra year of primary school will increase a girl's future earnings by 10 to 20%. An extra year of secondary school will increase them by 15 to 25%.[3]

... she will be healthier and live longer.

FACT

Girls between 10 and 14 are five times more likely to die in pregnancy or childbirth than women between 20 and 24.[4]

There are many obstacles to educating girls. There are many stories of girls who have found ways to overcome them.

The girls on the following pages make up the tiniest tip of an enormous iceberg. What happens to them, and to all the other girls who want to go to school, will determine how our global story continues—and how our world will or will not change.

Meet some of these girls and you will begin to grasp the power they have to change the world.

1 "... she is likely to marry ... has 2.2 fewer children." Data from Ruth Levine, Cynthia B. Lloyd, Margaret Greene, and Caren Grown, *A Global Investment & Action Agenda: A Girls Count Report on Adolescent Girls,* Center for Global Development, Girls Count, 2009, http://www.cgdev.org/files/15154_file_GC_2009_Final_web.pdf.

2 "... there will be fewer infant ... the baby of a mother over 19." Data from "Why is giving special attention to adolescents important for achieving Millennium Development Goal 5?", World Health Organization, 2008, http://www.who.int/maternal_child_adolescent/events/2008/mdg5/adolescent _preg.pdf.

3 "... she will be able to get a better ... will increase them by 15 to 25%." Data from George Psacharopoulos and Harry Anthony Patrinos, "Returns to /Investment in Education: A Further Update," World Bank. *Education Economics* 12.2 (2002): 111–34, http://siteresources.worldbank.org/INTDEBTDEPT Resources/468980-1170954447788/3430000-1273248341332/20100426_16.pdf.

4 "... she will be healthier ... women between 20 and 24." Data from "Women Leaders in Latin America and the Caribbean Seek New Alliances to Reduce Maternal Mortality," United Nations Population Fund, May 31, 2010, http://www.unfpa.org/news/women-leaders-latin-america-and-caribbean-seek-new -alliances-reduce-maternal-mortality.

EVERY GIRL HAS A STORY.

Peru: Jamileth is a Rubik's Cube whiz.

India: Neelam plans to be a nurse.

Haiti: Nerlande gives her friends great advice.

Sierra Leone: Sarah is inquisitive.

Nepal: Sita looks out for her little sister.

India: Nazma loves ghost stories.

Sierra Leone: Pricilla knows her Shakespeare.

Peru: Clarita won an award for writing.

Uganda: Lydia lives with her grandmother.

Haiti: Wendjie likes to play basketball.

Egypt: Hoda wants to be a teacher.

India:
Ruksana loves to draw and paint.

Sierra Leone:
M'ballu is a fashionista.

Ethiopia:
Banchiayehu is close to her brother.

Cambodia:
Sopatt loves to read to her mother.

Nepal:
Asha is extremely brave.

Cambodia:
Sokha expresses herself through dance.

Ethiopia:
Azmera is funny and shy.

Egypt:
Yasmin has a strong sense of humor.

Peru:
Senna could rule any poetry slam.

Sierra Leone:
Mariama is a radio talk-show host.

Haiti:
Wadley calls her favorite doll Ashley.

Nepal:
Suma sings with a strong, clear voice.

PART TWO

THE STORIES

Carrying water, Ethiopia.

You now have a sense of *why* it is so important to educate girls. And yes, it is absolutely as important to educate boys. But around the world, girls face obstacles to education that boys don't face—and boys are educated at a much higher rate than girls. So *what* are these obstacles keeping girls out of school? And *how* do most of them stem from the root problems of gender discrimination and poverty?

Gender discrimination occurs when a woman or girl is seen as not having the same value as a man or boy, and therefore is not given the same rights, opportunities, or treatment. This plays out in many ways; some may seem

"When I saw other children with books in their hands on their way to school, I felt a fire inside me."
—Hoda, Egypt

No Access to Education

Child Marriage

Sexual Slavery

Early Childbirth

Violence Against Girls

Forced Labor

Poverty

Gender Discrimination

obvious, while others may be harder to detect. When it comes to education, gender discrimination rears its ugly head in the basic idea that girls don't need school as much as boys do.

Poverty plays a crucial role in girls' lack of education. When people are so poor that basic necessities—enough food to eat, clothes to wear, a place to live—are a struggle, it is easy to see how paying for school becomes a luxury that is not an option, especially if you are a girl.

Poverty and gender discrimination go hand in hand in many places for complex reasons: cultural, religious, and economic. In some countries, even when a family can find enough money to pay school fees, they may have to choose which of their children they can spare. Often, the boys are sent, while the girls are kept home to work—carrying water, caring for younger siblings, collecting firewood, tending livestock—or sent to work for someone else. And marrying girls off at a young age to have one less mouth to feed is frequent in poverty-stricken regions. The girls might even be sold.

As we explore these obstacles to education, you'll see that a lot of them overlap. But all over the world, girls are overcoming them.

"My family needed me to work in the fields and the school fees were too expensive, but my heart was sick about it."

—Douaa, Egypt

Suma, Nepal.

MODERN-DAY SLAVERY

*Slavery is not legal anywhere,
but it happens everywhere.*

NOT A THING OF THE PAST

When you hear the word "slavery," it may conjure up images and ideas of the 1400s, when Portuguese traders first brought slaves from West Africa into Europe, or the 1600s, when Massachusetts became the first British colony to legalize slavery. You may know that slavery is far older than that. It began in the very first city, Mesopotamia, in 6800 BC, when captured enemies were made slaves. It was not until the 1700s that efforts to abolish slavery began to take hold in parts of the western world. Even though those abolitionist efforts made great strides, slavery is not a thing of the past.

Slavery not only still exists, it is thriving.

There are more than twenty million victims of slavery today—a higher number of enslaved people than at any other time in world history. Why? For one thing, there

"I feel strong when someone loves me."
—Marilu, Peru

A survivor of human trafficking, Marilu was safely in a shelter when Girl Rising interviewed her.

are more of us living on the planet than ever before. Our planet now has more people than our limited resources can support. This creates poverty, and poverty makes people vulnerable to those who will prey upon them. It can also make them desperate enough to see no other way to survive than to participate in the slave trade. And even though slavery is a crime everywhere, many governments cannot, or do not, enforce their laws.

Human trafficking is a modern term for the slave trade. Most trafficking victims are used for labor or sex. There are various other terms for modern-day slavery, including bonded labor, forced labor, *restavèk,* and *kamlari.* No matter what it is called, it means the same thing: human beings forced to work against their will. Sometimes they receive a little money; sometimes they work merely for bare necessities.

Children everywhere are vulnerable; 33 percent of enslaved people are under the age of eighteen. And two out of three of these victims are girls. Professor Benjamin Lawrance, an expert in human trafficking at Rochester Institute of Technology, said, "There has never been a period of time where child slavery didn't take place." He was referring to Africa in particular, but child trafficking exists in many parts of the world.

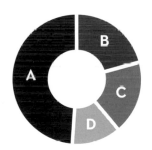

TRAFFICKING VICTIMS
by Gender / Age[1]

A. Women: **49%**   C. Men: **18%**
B. Girls: **21%**   D. Boys: **12%**

FORMS OF EXPLOITATION
Among Trafficking Victims[2]

A. Forced Labor: **40%**
B. Sexual Slavery: **53%**
C. Other: **7%**

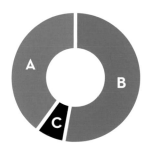

1 UNODC Report, "Global Report on Trafficking in Persons," 2014, p. 5.
2 UNODC Report, "Global Report on Trafficking in Persons," 2014, p. 9.

RANI

FROM INDIA

A WORLD OF DARKNESS

Rani was eighteen years old when the *Girl Rising* team interviewed her. The video of that interview is striking, as all that is visible of her is the back of her head, her black hair neatly pulled back, pinned with barrettes. This vantage point is to protect Rani's identity so she can tell her story freely, without fear. Rani is not her real name.

Girl Rising producer Martha Adams took notes during Rani's interview and wrote that Rani was "funny and animated" and "lights up the room." For many years, though, Rani lived in a world of darkness. Her parents sold her to a stranger as a servant when she was eight. When she was ten, Rani was sold again—this time she was forced to work as a prostitute for five long years. She tried to escape a few times and was punished cruelly for her attempts. Finally, Rani managed to flee and ended up in the care of an NGO (a nongovernmental organization; NGOs are organizations not operating for profit and not associated with any government) called Prerana, which works to stop human trafficking. But Rani was so shattered by what had happened to her that she did not trust anyone. She was aggressive and angry, and fought the people at Prerana. Eventually, Rani began to trust them. She spoke with counselors and started taking classes—learning computer skills, studying language, and even participating in a training program with a hotel group.

Rani is bright and her progress was swift. When she first arrived, she could not read or write a single word. Within six months, she had learned both the English and Indian alphabets and was able to start reading the newspaper. She also began teaching younger children their letters. At the time Martha Adams met her, Rani had been at Prerana for three years.

By then, Rani was effervescent. She talked a mile a minute. She was vital and strong. This resilience is common among girls who manage to find a way out of dreadful situations and into programs dedicated to helping them heal and recover.

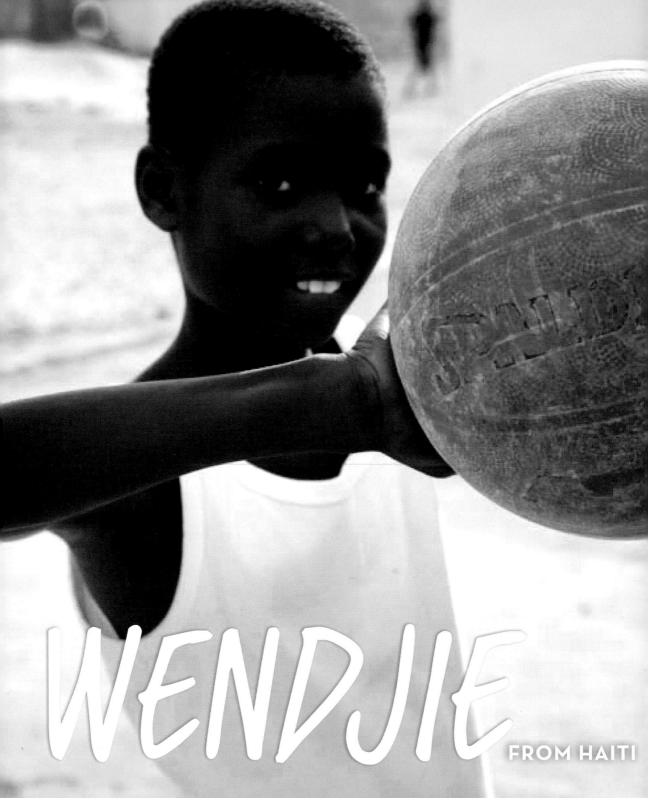

WENDJIE

FROM HAITI

"THEY CLEAN YOUR HOUSE FOR NOTHING"

Wendjie lives in Haiti. She was nine when Girl Rising producer Martha Adams met her at the Centre of Action for Development (CAD), an organization that helps street children and orphans. Wendjie is an only child, and both of her parents died in a terrible earthquake in Haiti in 2010. Many people lost loved ones in the disaster, or were separated from them and unable to find them in the chaos. One man spotted Wendjie and took her home with him, putting her to work in his household. He had her do chores six days a week and didn't let her go to school. After about a year, the man took her to the police station to become her legal guardian, but Wendjie told the police she did not want to stay with him. That's how she ended up at CAD, once again happy to be going to school. She is a good student and loves to play basketball.

In Haiti, some children—usually daughters—of parents too poor to care for them are sent to live with other families to work as unpaid servants. These children are called *restavèks,* which means "to stay with," in Creole. Orphans are also at high risk of becoming *restavèks.* Sometimes *restavèks* are treated fairly and kindly, and sent to school. Most often, though, they work ten to fourteen hours a day, suffering from malnutrition and abuse.

One United Nations worker said this about *restavèks:* "Many of them are treated like animals. They are second-class citizens, little slaves. You feed them a little and they clean your house for nothing." Despite the fact that child slavery is illegal in Haiti, as is employing anyone under the age of fifteen, the number of *restavèks* continues to grow. There are between 150,000 and 500,000 *restavèks* in Haiti at any given time. Some are as young as five years old. Two-thirds of them are girls.

Author and activist Nicholas Kristof visited Haiti in 2013 to interview *restavèks* with the assistance of an organization called Restavek Freedom. Through them, he met Marilaine, a thirteen-year-old girl who was forced to work in a stranger's home. When she tried to run away, she was beaten. Kristof also met a twelve-year-old girl who worked from four in the morning until late at night and was physically abused by everyone in her new "family." Other journalists have encountered *restavèks* who endure similar treatment—they must gather wood, carry water, cook, and clean, from the wee hours of the morning until long into the night. And after all that hard

After the 2010 earthquake in Haiti, tent camps like these housed hundreds of thousands of displaced people.

work, they are often fed scraps and not given the little schooling that was promised their parents in exchange for their children's labor.

It can be difficult for those who do not live with poverty to truly understand how these situations can happen to families, but trying to imagine being in their shoes can be a powerful way to empathize. Dr. Arthur Fournier, from the University of Miami, has been doing health work in Haiti for fifteen years, and has seen why some families have resorted to turning their children into *restavèks*. He said, "The parents aren't bad parents. These are the survival choices they have to make."

This still from the *Girl Rising* film portrays a young *kamlari*.

A MASTER HAS COMPLETE POWER

In an area of southwestern Nepal, where the Tharu people live, a similar practice of bonded labor called *kamlari* has existed quietly for generations. The majority of *kamlari* are girls, but boys can be bonded, too. Each January, the annual Maghe Festival celebrates the end of winter and the beginning of a new year. In Tharu tradition, village leaders are selected, and families gather to celebrate with feasts of pig, duck, spinach, yams, and fudge made of roasted sesame seeds and molasses. Maghe also marks the time when families review their year together, assigning responsibilities for the coming year and discussing past mistakes. For some of these families, a much darker scene is unfolding, in conversations about which masters their daughters will be sent to for a year of servitude. These families know that *kamlari* brokers are at the festival to buy girls for their masters.

Often, the agreement made is for a small sum of money—although that sum may mean their survival. Other times payment is only food and clothing for their children. *Kamlari* may be sent hundreds of miles from their homes, and only allowed to visit their families once or twice a year—if at all. Although the practice of *kamlari* has been illegal since 2000, it is still happening to thousands of girls each year.

A master has complete power over his *kamlari*. He can—and often does—abuse that power. *Kamlari* commonly work from sunup to sundown, and are often treated horribly, enduring emotional, physical, and sexual abuse. And while all a girl may think about is going back home at the end of a year, many are not returned to their families. Even if they are, it may only be to repeat the nightmare and be sold or given away to new masters.

Manjita was nine when her father sold her for the equivalent of twenty-five dollars and sent her more than one hundred miles away. Her younger sister was also sold—their parents did not have enough money to raise either of them. Manjita worked from four a.m. until midnight, cleaning, washing dishes, and cooking for the policeman to whom she was sold, and for his relatives. When she couldn't keep up with the work, the policeman's wife beat her with pots and pans. "I was so scared, I couldn't even cry in front of them," Manjita remembered.

After three years of enduring this, when Manjita was twelve, the Nepal Youth Foundation (NYF) intervened. The NYF became aware of the *kamlari* practice in 2000 and launched a campaign alerting and educating people about it. They began to find ways to rescue girls. In Manjita's case, by offering to fund their education and give them counseling and career training to help them overcome the trauma of having been *kamlari,* the NYF convinced their father to free both of his daughters. Since then, the NYF has rescued more than 12,000 girls.

Former *kamlari* girls, Nepal.

ASHA

FROM NEPAL

"A STAGGERINGLY RESILIENT BUNCH"

Girl Rising met several former *kamlari* girls through the NYF and another organization called Room to Read. Room to Read began in Nepal, and now has programs dedicated to gender equality and literacy in many countries. When *Girl Rising* director Richard Robbins was in Nepal interviewing girls for the film, he jotted this down in his field notes: "It's pretty hard to get your head around what it must be like to be sent away from your family at eight or nine to basically be a slave. They are a staggeringly resilient bunch, full of life and hope in spite of the hardship they've endured."

Asha was one of the girls the film crew interviewed. When Richard and Martha Adams met Asha, she had been freed for three years, but it was still clearly difficult for her to talk about her life as a *kamlari*. She stopped several times to take a breath, wipe away tears, and try to find the words to describe her experience.

Asha was twelve when she was sent far from home, to Kathmandu, the capital city of Nepal. Each day, she was worked until the point of exhaustion, and physically abused. Asha waited for her visit to her parents after a year's labor, but that promise was taken away just as the date drew near. That promise had kept her going. She begged to be able to see her parents, but her master refused. So Asha made a daring decision. With only one hundred rupees in her pocket—less than two dollars—she ran away, and somehow managed to find her way back to her village.

But at the end of Asha's race home to freedom, angry parents awaited her, upset with her for leaving her master. Rather than let her go back to school, they tried to keep her home, urging their son to go instead. He had no interest.

Eventually, through Room to Read, Asha was enrolled in school. When Richard and Martha spoke with her, she was taking a life skills class and studying at the eighth-grade level. They asked her a question they had asked other girls they interviewed: If you could take an airplane ride anywhere in the world, where would you go?

Her answer momentarily baffled Richard:

"And so this girl, when offered an imaginary plane ride to anywhere, sat and thought for a long moment. Then she answered that she would take a flight 'to education.' I confess I thought she must have misunderstood the question. I did not believe that she could form this incredible metaphor. But I was wrong. She knew exactly what she was saying."

Imagine being this clear and firm, after such an experience.

When a practice like *kamlari* is embedded into the lives of a people for generations, it can be difficult to break free of it and to envision another way of life. But Asha could picture a better future and, luckily, Nepalese social workers from Room to Read were there to help her. Asha now hopes to become a social worker herself and work with disadvantaged children.

Asha, studying.

SITA

FROM NEPAL

THEY HAD NO OTHER CHOICE

Along with Asha, Girl Rising met Sita through Room to Read. She was twenty years old when Martha Adams talked with her about her experience as a *kamlari*. Sita was sold when she was ten, after she had been in school for about three years. She was a good student. Unlike seven million Nepalese people, Sita already knew how to read and write. She was soft-spoken and articulate.

Sita's family always believed in educating her. It had not entered Sita's mind that she would ever become a *kamlari*. Her parents hoped that they would never have to send her into bonded labor, but they were so poor, the family was close to starving. Sita remembers her younger siblings crying from hunger. By the time Sita turned ten, her parents felt they had no other choice.

Sita's mother—who was also bonded as a *kamlari* when she was a girl—was heartbroken. The day before Sita was to leave, she held her daughter all through the night, crying.

In the morning, instead of taking the exams she had studied for, Sita was sent away. She knew no one in the new village, and her master kept her isolated, not allowing her to go beyond the fence barricading his house. She worked from four a.m. to ten p.m. each day, and was given just two sparse meals a day. In exchange for her labor, her family could farm the land they were living on, which was owned by her master. Sita was only allowed to see her family once a year, at the Maghe Festival. After a visit, going back with her master was always difficult.

It was four years before Sita was returned home for good, after working for a few different masters. Through a partnership between Room to Read and another NGO—Friends of Needy Children (FNC)—Sita was able to go back to school, her education supported through the twelfth grade.

SUMA

FROM NEPAL

"UNLUCKY GIRL"

Suma is from the Tharu community in Nepal. She has four brothers and two sisters, and all but one of them have been *kamlari*. Suma's parents were bonded when they were children, too.

About being in a master's house, Suma says, "It's similar to when you see a dog on a leash being walked. . . . You're basically captive in the house . . . and you cannot leave. . . . To be a *kamlari* is to lead the life of slavery in the house."

The first time Suma was bonded as a *kamlari,* she was only six. Her parents did not even trade her for money, but so she could have enough food to eat, somewhere to live, and clothes to wear that year. The day Suma's master came to get her, she was too young to understand what was happening, or where she was going.

When she arrived at her master's house, she was not sure what she was supposed to do, so she sat down in front of the house and leaned against a post. The mistress of the house yelled at her to stop being idle and sent her off to work. During that first year, she would rise at four a.m., clean the house, care for the children (even though she was only six years old herself), go out with a basket and cut grass for their goats and buffalo, eat, wash the dishes, care for the children again, and so on, until about nine p.m.

At the next two houses she was sent to, Suma worked at her chores from before sunup to after sundown. She also had to clean out the stalls for the cows and goats and go into the jungle alone to collect firewood.

The family in the first house had been unkind to her, but the treatment was far worse at her second master's. The mistress did not use her name; instead, she called Suma "Unlucky Girl." Suma remembers: "They made me sleep in the goat shed, and wear rags, and eat scraps from their dirty plates." She was also beaten. "I felt as though I was being treated like a dog."

Suma also suffered worse abuse that she will not bring herself to talk about in detail. When asked about what *kamlari* life can be like, though, she offered this: "What tends to happen is the masters feel they can do anything with the girls, and they often rape them and say, 'I want to make you my wife,' and treat them really badly."

IT WAS ALMOST A HAPPY ENDING

Suma's courage and strength to respond to questions about such a dark time is impressive. She is smart and well-spoken. Her ability to express so much now is a direct result of the education she eventually received.

At first, that help came while Suma was living with her third master. The family there was kind, and she was well fed and clothed. They also happened to have a lodger named Bimal Sir, who was a teacher. He convinced Suma's master to allow her to take a night class taught by social workers that was offered especially for *kamlari*. The girls learned how to read and write after their day's work was finished. They also had a chance to talk about what *kamlari* life was like for them. As they talked, the girls began to realize that *kamlari* was akin to slavery. Suma had turned twelve by then. She had been a *kamlari* for six years.

After Suma was able to read and write well enough, Bimal Sir enrolled her in his school and brought her books so she could study after her daily work was done. Even though she wasn't able to attend classes during the day, she learned at her own pace and sat for exams. Suma progressed quickly.

Meanwhile, the social workers teaching classes were also quite busy gathering information to set the *kamlari* girls free. They went house by house, village by village, asking if there were *kamlari* there, and recording the names. Suma tells what happened next: "One day, a social worker, Sita-didi, came to talk to my master. Sita-didi was educated, and could speak very confidently. She told my master that he was breaking the law by keeping me as a *kamlari*. She talked about the law against bonded labor, and the law about children's rights, and the law on labor rights, and

A still from the *Girl Rising* film depicting *kamlari* girls studying after working all day.

the law against domestic violence, and also the law against trafficking. And she demanded that he set me free. My master said no; once made, a bond couldn't be broken. But Sita-didi didn't give up. She kept arguing—and in the end, she won. She led me home to my mother and father."

It was almost a happy ending. But the master went to her parents' house several times and took her back. Her parents did not protest. Suma said, "I wanted to fight with my mother and father, I wanted to demand that they let me stay at home and go to school, like my brother. But when I thought about how much they had suffered . . . I loved them, and that made me weak. I couldn't fight with them."

But Sita-didi fought on Suma's behalf. Each time, Sita-didi returned to Suma's master's house and argued with him. Finally, Suma's parents agreed to help, and to figure out a way to afford to keep her at home. Suma was soon given a scholarship by Room to Read so she could attend school full-time through their Girls'

Education program. Suma is grateful for the change in her life that school offers. She doesn't waste a minute there. "I love all my teachers. . . . Everything they say is so interesting. I attend every class and take part in every after-school activity: even quiz contests and debates, even football."

"OTHER GIRLS LIKE ME NEED TO BE RESCUED"

Suma has an intimate understanding of the power of being educated. "Education is like the light in our eyes. We don't know anything until we get an education, we don't even know where to go. . . . It's not just in order to have a job, it's also something you have to do for yourself and others can never steal it—it always stays with you."

Suma began spending some of her time helping *kamlari* girls who are not yet as lucky as she. "Even though the government has declared *kamlari* free," Suma says, "there are thousands of friends like me who are still suffering." Suma has done for others what Sita-didi did for her.

Suma says, "I want to work in an organization for women's rights. I'd like to raise a voice about injustices against women. Other girls like me need to be rescued and to be helped in the ways that I've been helped."

Many girls in similar situations echo this sentiment—and it is a real reflection of the ripple effect. After interviewing more than twenty former *kamlari* girls in Nepal, Richard Robbins wrote, "The girls talked about the idea that they had to tell their communities and their parents the 'times are changing.' . . . They are passionate apostles for education. They are revolutionaries. Now that they have been given this opportunity denied to their mothers and grandmothers and probably dozens of generations that have gone before, they want to be sure that they foster and spread the gift of education."

SUMA'S SONG

During Suma's first interview with Girl Rising, Martha Adams happened to ask her if she liked to sing. Instead of answering, Suma began to sing. A sad, faraway look came over her face. The pure, clear tone of her voice captivated the American filmmakers, although the meaning of the Nepalese lyrics escaped them. When Suma stopped, Martha told her it was one of the most beautiful things she had ever heard. Suma's pained face blossomed into a broad smile.

For Suma, singing had always been a way of coping. "As far back as I can remember," she said, "I loved to sing. I would sing as I worked, I would sing as I rested, I would sing all the time, even though everyone scolded me: 'Can't you ever sit quietly?' I would sing about how much I wanted to go home."

Her songs changed as her challenges and feelings changed. "In this [second] house I sang about food, because I was always hungry." In the school where she took night classes, Suma "learned how to sing about freedom." Developing her language skills allowed her to express herself in ways she hadn't known. And when she was finally freed from her last master, in 2008, Suma wrote a song of sorrow for the plight of girls in her country. That was what she sang for Martha. Suma explained what the words meant, adding, "I wrote that song myself, and I wrote it not just for myself, but for thousands of other Nepali girls."

In March 2012, Girl Rising brought Suma to New York City to share her song with an audience of more than a thousand people gathered at Lincoln Center for the third annual Women in the World Summit. This event focuses on learning about what women's lives are like worldwide by listening to their firsthand stories.

Suma had never left Nepal before, but she bravely took the stage of the blackened theater. Video footage from when she first sang for Martha appeared on a huge screen above Suma, with a translation of her Nepali lyrics so the audience could follow the meaning as they listened. As a light came up on Suma, she first joined in with her video self, and then took over singing the song live for the Lincoln Center crowd, while they listened intently. When her last note hung in the air, the audience burst into cheers and applause. Suma smiled, proud that she was heard, gratified that she was understood.

Suma's Song

Thoughtless were my mother and father
They gave birth to a daughter
They gave birth to a daughter

Did you want to see me suffer, Mother?
Did you want to see me suffer, Father?

Then why did you give birth to a daughter?
Then why did you give birth to a daughter?

My brothers go to school to study
While I, unfortunate, slave at a master's house
While I, unfortunate, slave at a master's house
Abused every day by the landlord's wife

It's a hard life, being beaten every day
It's a hard life, being beaten every day

Thoughtless were my mother and father
They gave birth to a daughter
They gave birth to a daughter

Suma performing her song at the Women in the World Summit, New York City.

Aseya, Ethiopia.

CHILD MARRIAGE

In developing nations,
the number one
cause of death for girls
ages fifteen to nineteen
is not disease.

It is not hunger.

It is not war.

It is childbirth.

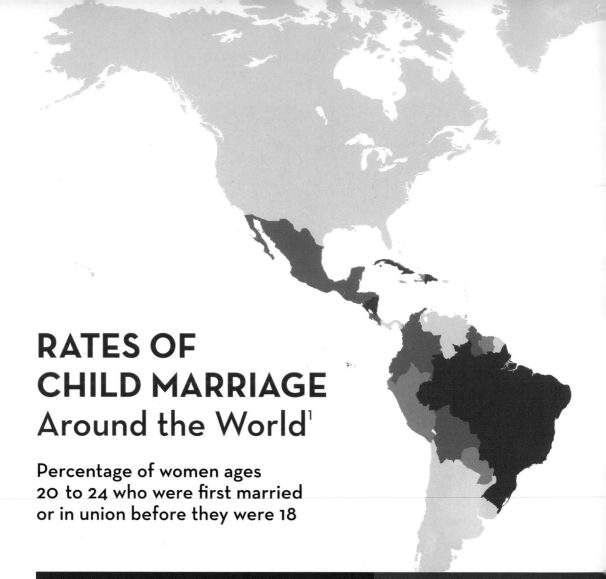

RATES OF
CHILD MARRIAGE
Around the World[1]

**Percentage of women ages
20 to 24 who were first married
or in union before they were 18**

Over 50%	36-50%
Bangladesh, Burkina Faso, Central African Republic, Chad, Guinea, Mali, Niger, South Sudan	Afghanistan, Brazil, Cameroon, Cuba, Democratic Republic of the Congo, Dominican Republic, Eritrea, Ethiopia, Gambia, India, Liberia, Madagascar, Malawi, Mozambique, Nepal, Nicaragua, Nigeria, Sierra Leone, Somalia, Uganda, United Republic of Tanzania, Zambia

 Less than 2% or no data available*

1 State of the World's Children 2015, UNICEF, Table 9: pp. 84–89. http://www.unicef.org/publications/files/SOWC_2015_Summary_and_Tables.pdf.
* Country List in Appendix.

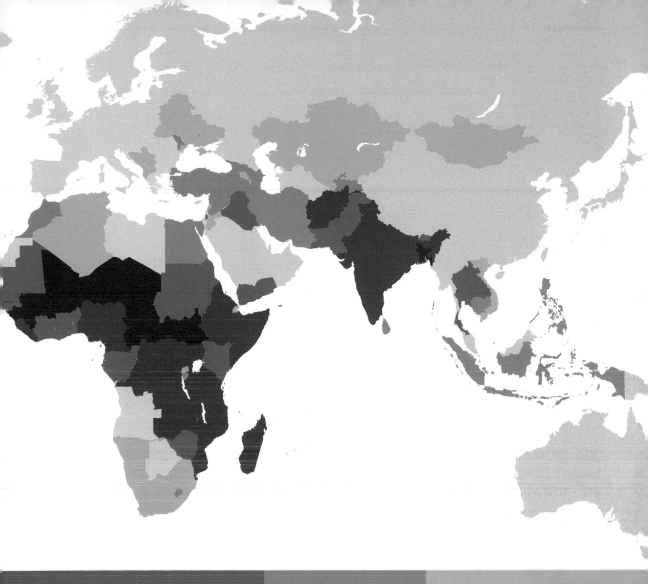

21-35%

Belize, Benin, Bhutan, Bolivia, Colombia, Comoros, Congo, Costa Rica, Côte d'Ivoire, Ecuador, El Salvador, Equatorial Guinea, Gabon, Ghana, Guatemala, Guinea-Bissau, Guyana, Honduras, Iraq, Kenya, Lao People's Democratic Republic, Marshall Islands, Mauritania, Mexico, Nauru, Pakistan, Sao Tome and Principe, Senegal, Solomon Islands, State of Palestine, Sudan, Thailand, Togo, Vanuatu, Yemen, Zimbabwe

11-20%

Azerbaijan, Burundi, Cabo Verde, Cambodia, Egypt, Georgia, Haiti, Indonesia, Iran, Kiribati, Lesotho, Morocco, Paraguay, Peru, Philippines, Republic of Moldova, Sri Lanka, Suriname, Syrian Arab Republic, Tajikistan, Timor-Leste, Turkey

2-10%

Albania, Algeria, Armenia, Belarus, Bosnia and Herzegovina, Djibouti, Jamaica, Jordan, Kazakhstan, Kyrgyzstan, Lebanon, Maldives, Mongolia, Montenegro, Namibia, Rwanda, Saint Lucia, Serbia, South Africa, Swaziland, Former Yugoslav Republic of Macedonia, Tonga, Trinidad and Tobago, Tunisia, Tuvalu, Ukraine, Uzbekistan, Viet Nam

Azmera (left) avoided an arranged
marriage and is now in school.

What does your future hold? Do you want a career? A family? Will you go to college before you get married? Pursue your dreams before you have children? Will these choices be up to *you* to make?

Child marriage *is* the future for millions of girls around the world. Fourteen million girls under eighteen will be married this year. That's thirty-eight thousand girls married today. That's thirteen girls in the last thirty seconds.

Over the next ten years, if nothing changes, 140 million girls will be married young. These are usually forced marriages—the girls are not given a choice.

Most countries have laws in place that set a minimum age of marriage at eighteen. But many countries, including the United States, Canada, several European nations, and others, allow for exceptions with parental or court consent. And in some developing nations, marriage laws are not followed or enforced. In July 2013, Nigeria amended its constitution with a legal loophole that resulted in legalizing marriage for girls under the age of eighteen—a backward step. Child marriage is most common in South Asia and Sub-Saharan Africa, but also occurs around the world, including in African nations above the Sahara. To get around whatever laws do exist, child marriages often take place in secret, and the plan is kept from the bride herself until the last possible moment.

THE PRICE FOR A DAUGHTER

In a village in western Kenya, a teenage girl is about to be married. She was not told about her wedding until it was time for the ceremony so she couldn't run away. When the men from the tribe come to get her, she kicks and screams, trying to fight them off. But her struggle is in vain; her father has promised her in marriage. The price her family is paid for their daughter? Twenty goats, ten cows, and a couple of camels.

The parents of a girl from Zambia told her she "was no longer their responsibility. . . . When a stranger paid a bride price to my parents, I had no say in the matter." She wanted to become a nurse, but now spends her time taking care of her husband's home. "My husband won't allow me to further my studies," she told BBC reporter Nomsa Maseko. With no money of her own, and the knowledge that her parents will not take her back, she has little power to change her fate.

A girl's world changes abruptly and dramatically from the moment she marries. Childhood ends and a life of labor begins. She is often cut off from her family, isolated from loved ones. She is often subject to domestic violence, especially when the husband is significantly older. And child marriage nearly always results in her dropping out of school—or never having a chance to go at all.

In turn, a lack of education increases the likelihood that a girl will live in poverty. She will not be able to read and write, or support herself, or raise her children in better circumstances.

And the births of her children will generally happen in quick succession, as one prominent reason for child marriage in many developing nations is the idea that a girl's primary worth is her ability to reproduce. Child marriage equals children giving birth to children. This is why such marriages also put girls' health—and even their lives—in danger. The physical risks of early sexual activity and childbearing are high. Child brides have a pregnancy death rate (called maternal mortality) double that of women in their twenties, as their bodies are not yet developed enough to give birth successfully.

EDUCATION
Changes Lives

Girls with 8 years of education are 4 times less likely to be married as children.[1]

Girls from poor families are nearly twice as likely to marry before 18 as girls from wealthier families.[2]

A child born to a literate mother is 50% more likely to survive past the age of 5.[3]

1 "Girls with 8 years . . . as children." Data from Barbara S. Mensch, Susheela Singh, and John B. Casterline, "Trends in the Timing of First Marriage Among Men and Women in the Developing World," in Cynthia B. Lloyd, Jere R. Behrman, Nelly P. Stromquist, and Barney Cohen (eds.), *The Changing Transitions to Adulthood in Developing Countries: Selected Studies,* Washington, DC: National Academies Press, 2005: 118–171.

2 "Girls from poor . . . wealthier families." Data from *Knot Ready: Lessons from India on Delaying Marriage for Girls,* International Center for Research on Women (ICRW), 2008: 9, http://www.icrw. org/files/publications/Knot-Ready-Lessons-from-India-on-Delaying-Marriage-for-Girls.pdf.

3 "A child born to . . . age of 5." Data from *Education Counts: Towards the Millennium Development Goals,* United Nations Educational, Scientific and Cultural Organization (UNESCO), 2011, http://unesdoc.unesco.org/images/0019/001902/190214e.pdf.

"SNATCH UP THE GIRL . . . AND RUN"

In some places, crises such as food shortages, natural disasters, or war can exacerbate the problem of child marriage. This is happening in Niger, which already has the highest rate of child marriage in the world. Djanabou Mahonde, UNICEF's head of child protection, said, "The fear is, if the food crisis continues, that more parents will use marriage as a survival strategy and that we'll see more girls married before the age of fifteen." In Nepal, after two major quakes devastated that nation in April and May 2015, thousands of girls were orphaned, were separated from loved ones, or no longer had a safe place to be during the day because hundreds of schools were destroyed. These girls became instantly more vulnerable to trafficking, as well as to being married off, as parents scrambled to find some way to give their daughters a more stable future.

In Syria, a civil war that began in 2011 has resulted in several million Syrians fleeing to neighboring countries. Jordan took in hundreds of thousands of Syrians. Life in refugee camps can be quite dangerous for girls, and child marriage can be seen as a way to protect girls from being sexually assaulted. One worker at an organization that offers medical care in the camps said, "These families feel marriage would be the best option for a girl growing up as a refugee." Since before the war, the number of Syrian girls marrying under the age of eighteen has more than doubled.

Some parents also reason that marrying a Syrian daughter to a Jordanian will help ensure her future in her new country. But these plans can backfire. One Syrian refugee married off her fifteen-year-old daughter Jazia in order to protect her, only to learn that Jazia's new husband was beating her.

In a farming community in northern India, three girls took part in a clandestine late-night marriage ceremony. The thirteen- and fifteen-year-old sisters were old enough to understand what was happening to them. But their five-year-old niece

Rajani, in a pretty pink shirt for the occasion, had no idea that she was being given away to a husband. At any moment, a police officer could have interrupted these weddings and arrested those responsible, but no one came to rescue the girls.

To people outside of these cultures, such marriages can seem outrageous, a clear-cut wrong that needs righting. As *National Geographic* journalist Cynthia Gorney writes, "The outsider's impulse toward child bride rescue scenarios can be overwhelming: Snatch up the girl, punch out the nearby adults, and run. Just make it stop." But it's never that simple. This practice is tied up in long-held cultural beliefs and traditions, as well as economic constraint. A marriage can settle a debt among families, bring much-needed money into the house, and reduce the number of people to support.

"IT'S BEEN DONE THIS WAY FOR GENERATIONS"

Maaza Mengiste is an Ethiopian American writer who wrote the Ethiopian story in the *Girl Rising* film. In an interview with the producers, she talked about some of the underlying reasons that childhood marriage exists in Ethiopia. The reasons are similar in many nations:

"Parents feel like they have to marry their daughters off early. . . . It's what the mothers experienced, it's what their mothers experienced—it's been done this way for generations, and it becomes thought of as a cultural thing, as customary. But the reason . . . is really the nature of economics and the financial hardships on the family. The family feels they need to send a girl off to another man's home so that he can give her a better life, he can take care of her. Sometimes there's a dowry or there's an exchange of money involved in this, and so the family that sends this daughter off to get married will then get money, cattle, something else in exchange. So it becomes a financial trade as well as . . . in the best situations, a better future for the girl—*they think.*"

AMINA

FROM AFGHANISTAN

A GIRL WAS NO USE TO HER

Afghanistan has laws in place against both forced marriage and marrying girls under sixteen, but that doesn't stop both from occurring regularly. Even shelters set up to protect child brides who manage to escape have significant challenges. In Kabul, Afghanistan, for example, one shelter that cares for both child brides and their children faces serious dangers while trying to carry out this work. In June 2010, CNN reporter Nic Robertson was at the shelter, waiting to interview a new arrival, when he found out that her family was threatening to take her back, even if it meant marching their whole village to the city to protest. Not only was this one girl's life at risk should she be returned to her husband, but the protest would put everyone at the shelter in harm's way. These ongoing threats make it difficult for shelters to continue helping child brides who flee.

There are so many stories of girls being forced to marry as children that they could fill hundreds of books, even though lawmakers and dedicated organizations are making progress around the globe on this issue. Remarkably, progress is also happening because of the resolve of the girls themselves. Many take matters into their own hands. Just speaking up is a huge step forward, regardless of the outcome. To have a voice and to be heard is to gain power.

The Girl Rising team visited girls' schools in Afghanistan in the hopes of finding one girl brave enough to speak about pursuing an education. The producers saw a variety of schools—some rural with no building or supplies; others in more populated areas with proper desks, a small library, and a few blackboards. They met teachers in training sessions, who continued to work hard while the camera was on, even though they were wary of being shown on film. They also met several girls whose stories were compelling—girls who want to be doctors, engineers, or teachers—but ultimately were either too afraid to talk or a family member did not want them to share their story because of the dangers associated with speaking up.

Then they met Amina (not her real name). Amina's experience is similar to that of hundreds of other girls in Afghanistan. What is exceptional, however, is her courage. Amina was intent on speaking with Afghan writer Zarghuna ("Zari") Kargar for the *Girl Rising* film. Zari is the author of a book called *Dear Zari: The Secret Lives of the Women of Afghanistan.* Zari knew that to speak out is to bring shame to the honor of your family, a crime often punishable by death. Despite the danger, Amina was willing to be shown on camera as long as she was completely covered. It was critically important to her to be heard. Ultimately, the film's director, Richard Robbins, decided the best way to keep her identity a secret was to hire an actress

This actress played the role of Amina in the *Girl Rising* film to protect the real girl's identity.

to portray Amina in the film. The home that was shown was a set, and the chapter was shot in a different country. Everyone involved was careful not to reveal Amina's identity, or details of where she lived. This is her story.

When Amina's mother learned her newborn was a girl, she cried. A girl was no use to her. Worse, a girl was a burden. Amina's father was a proud but poor farmer, making barely enough to feed his family. From the time she was three, Amina was put to work. She woke before dawn, fetched water, cleaned the house, washed the clothes and the dishes, collected firewood, fed chickens, and carried her siblings on her back until they were old enough to walk. She learned early that women were destined to live lives of servitude.

For a few years, Amina did get a taste of what it was like to receive an education. At first she learned to read and write on an old blackboard fixed to the trunk of a tree. Then her parents allowed her to go to a real school. Amina was grateful, for she knew that many Afghan girls weren't allowed to go to school at all, weren't even allowed to step outside their homes.

A still from the *Girl Rising* film, the Afghanistan chapter about "Amina."

"A VERY DARK PERIOD"

Things in Afghanistan weren't always this way. When writer Zari Kargar was growing up there, Kabul was known as a center of education, a university city. Although she used to be in an arranged marriage, Zari did not marry until she was twenty-one, and her education was not sacrificed. Her four sisters were all educated, too. At that time, women held positions in the parliament, and were doctors, engineers, and lawyers. But then, Zari said, "Afghanistan went through a very dark period." She is referring to the time when the Taliban was in control, roughly 1996 to 2001. Career women, including those in politics, were sent home. They weren't even free to walk the streets. Girls were forbidden to go to school.

"During that time," Zari said, "minds changed, opinions changed about women, about freedom of women." And in rural areas today, illiteracy rates are as high as 90 percent. Although there are nearly three million girls in school throughout Afghanistan now, each one takes a huge risk. Girls are poisoned, bombed, shot, stoned, disfigured, and burned for speaking out, for seeking equality, for wanting to be educated. In 2013, the United Nations reported a 28 percent increase in attacks against women in Afghanistan. And these are the *reported* numbers. Many incidents go unreported for fear of further violence.

Even if a girl is lucky enough to be sent to school, like Amina, it may be for only a little while—until her wedding. Amina was fourteen years old when her father arranged for her to be married to one of her cousins. Her mother approved, to Amina's despair. There would be no more school for her.

"A THIRST FOR CHANGE"

Amina knew the reasons for her situation. Her father was paid 250,000 Afghanis, roughly 5,000 U.S. dollars, for her. With this money, Amina's brother could buy a car and travel to a better job so he could send money back for the family. *Girl Rising* producer Amy Atkinson was struck by Amina's reaction as she recounted her story during their interview. "I note the rage in her fixed expression," Amy wrote in her notes. "She proudly blinks back tears, and repeats her refrain, 'He bought a car with the money, a car with my future.' In an instant, her anger turns to hurt, then despair. Her fire-eyes pool and then extinguish."

A classroom scene from the Afghanistan chapter in the film *Girl Rising*.

No one cared that Amina was married against her will. That she had a baby against her will. That she feels she will never be able to bring herself to see anything in that baby other than his father, the man who forced himself on her repeatedly, abused her, beat her. And still, she was lucky. Lucky not to have died giving birth in a country with one of the highest maternal mortality rates in the world.

Before her baby was even born, Amina's husband left them to find work in Iran, leaving her to raise their child in her in-laws' home. After three years, he returned for a few months, and then left them again. That was when Amina somehow convinced her parents to allow her to return to school.

Amina dreams of going to college and perhaps even meeting someone she can choose to love. Before her interview with Zari and Amy ended, she reminded them of the importance of not revealing her identity. If her husband ever found out, she told them, "He will kill me."

Though her situation was dire, when Amina spoke with Zari, she did not come across as a victim. She was smart. She knew that women in her country used to be educated. She knew about Afghan women who were role models. Although Amina may have been physically powerless, her voice was not.

"She had that passion, she had that fire in her to tell her story," Zari said. "Girls like Amina . . . you never know what kind of revolution she will lead. And I think women will be the ones who lead revolutions in Afghanistan. . . . You can see that there is an anger in her; there is a thirst for change. She wants to break those traditions, those rules."

It is the same in many places.

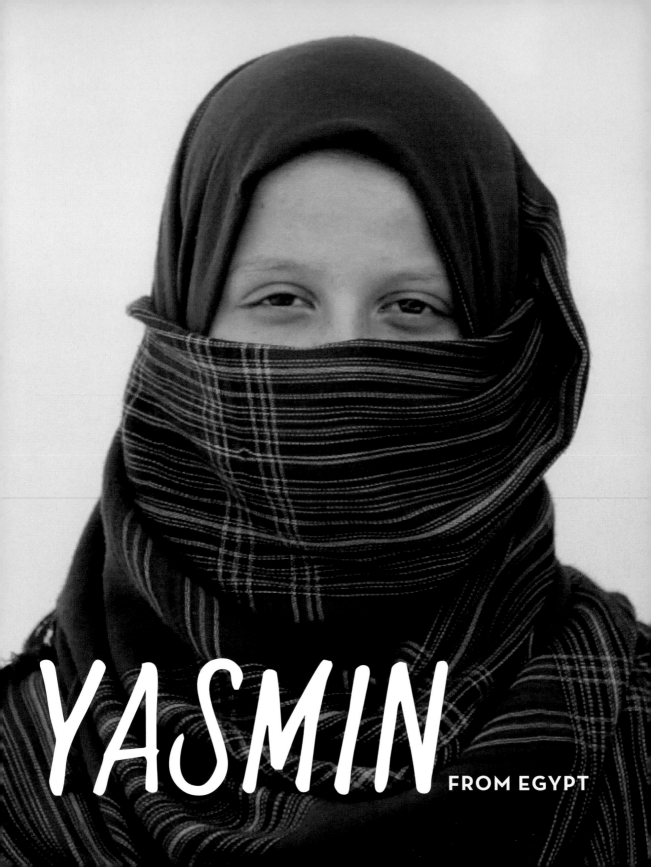

YASMIN

FROM EGYPT

"I'M GOING TO OPEN MY HEART TO YOU"

The harsh reality is that not all stories have a happy ending. Often, girls who don't have someone in their corner to make sure they find the help they need, or whose circumstances are too overwhelming, can't overcome their obstacles to education. Yet even then, a girl's spirit can still triumph. That is the case with a girl from Egypt we will call Yasmin. She is the youngest of four girls. They live with their mother in Cairo, have very little money, and all work to survive.

When I sat down to watch her interview footage, I already knew the basic facts of her painful story, but I was immediately struck by how often Yasmin smiled and giggled. She made funny faces at the camera, crossing her eyes, leaning forward and staring directly into the lens to make the photographer laugh. Her own laughing eyes flashed throughout the interview, a testimony to the strength of this girl. This girl who was raped. This girl whose mother later arranged for her to be married, as it was the only safe future she could imagine for her daughter. This girl who will likely never go to school.

Yasmin was interviewed for the *Girl Rising* film by Mona Eltahawy. Mona is an Egyptian American writer and activist. But right before she was to meet Yasmin and learn her story, Mona was in Tahrir Square in Cairo, Egypt, reporting on a protest against the then Egyptian president. Mona was arrested by the riot police. She was detained for twelve hours, during which time the police sexually and physically assaulted her, breaking her left arm and right wrist.

Mona Eltahawy talks with "Yasmin."

Mona considered returning to New York and postponing her interview with Yasmin, but decided against it. When they met, Yasmin looked at the two casts on Mona's wrists. She said to Mona, "I'm going to open my heart to you, and you're going to open your heart to me, and we're going to be really honest with each other, okay?"

Yasmin told Mona about the rape and the unusual circumstances that followed. They were unusual because in Egypt and many other places, sexual assault often goes unchallenged and unpunished. In fact, the victims are seen as tarnished or shameful and asked why they didn't fight back or resist. Mona knew this all too well. In the emergency room following her attack, she told the nurse what happened, and the nurse asked her those exact questions. The police, Mona said later, "rarely, if ever, intervene, or make arrests, or press charges. It was, after all, the riot police themselves who assaulted me."

Still, Yasmin and her mother went to the police, and they did receive help. Mona saw the roots of Yasmin's strength. "I know where she got this determination. . . . It's from her mom . . . that very clear sense of justice . . . to make sure justice is served and met, it was there."

Together, Yasmin and her mother told the police what happened, and the police arrested her attacker. As of this writing, the man was awaiting trial.

"HE FORCED ME"

In a different courthouse in Sana, Yemen, in April 2008, a young girl sat on a bench. Unaccompanied. Not even four feet tall, she had gone unnoticed for hours. Finally, the judge she was waiting for asked her what she was doing there. "I came to get a divorce," she said. Her name is Nujood, and at the time, she was ten years old.

Nujood's father had arranged for her to be married to a man in his thirties. Her father, who had sixteen children, said he was trying to protect her from being kidnapped and forced into an early marriage—a fate that had already befallen his eldest daughter. He also claimed that he asked the man not to sleep with Nujood, but to raise her until she was old enough to be a proper wife. The man denied having had any such conversation with Nujood's father. Nujood later told CNN, "When I married, I was afraid. I didn't want to leave home. I wanted to stay with my brothers, sisters, and mother. . . . I didn't want to sleep with him, but he forced me." He also began to beat her. Nujood's nights were filled with terror, her days with unending chores. She dreamed of being back with her family, playing with friends, writing her name on the blackboard at school.

When her husband finally let her visit her parents, she pleaded with them for help. Her father refused, saying that breaking the promise they had made to Nujood's husband meant dishonoring the family. Her mother was sympathetic: "When she told me what had been happening, my heart just burned for her." But she couldn't see a way out, telling her daughter, "All women must endure this; we have all gone through the same thing."

Nujood did not give up trying to make her family understand how unbearable her life had become. In a matter of months, she had been transformed from a child playing hide-and-seek with her friends to a battered wife. Finally, one relative suggested that she go to court and speak to a judge.

"TODAY I HAVE DECIDED TO SAY NO"

Nujood had seen courtrooms on television at a neighbor's house, and it gave her an idea. The next morning she summoned her courage. With the money her mother gave her to buy bread, she took a bus and then a taxi to get to the courthouse. Because she had been taken out of school so young, Nujood couldn't read, or write anything other than her name. The courthouse was a dizzying blur of signs and sounds and people bustling. She was afraid, but determined.

In the autobiography that Nujood wrote a few years later, she remembered what kept her going amid the chaos of the courthouse. "I'm a simple village girl. . . . I have always obeyed the orders of my fathers and brothers. Since forever, I have learned to say yes to everything. Today I have decided to say no."

After hearing her complaint, the judge was horrified. That a girl should be married so young was possible, he knew. But no girl had been brave enough to speak out and seek help. It took a while to figure out what to do with Nujood, since the court knew that sending her home would not be safe. Instead, another judge decided to take her home to his wife and family while the court came up with a plan.

"NO ONE HAS EVER SHOWN SO MUCH CONCERN FOR ME"

Shada Nasser, a Yemeni woman, is a well-known lawyer who fights for women's rights. She heard about Nujood's desire for a divorce and told the little girl she would represent her. She assured Nujood that she shouldn't be afraid. "No one has ever shown so much concern for me before," Nujood later wrote. Nasser got to work. She also notified the media. When Nujood's case was called, the courtroom was packed.

It was a scary time for Nujood. At just ten years old, she had to face her husband—a man who had terrified her repeatedly—in court. When asked how she was able to manage it, she replied, "I did it so that people would listen and think again about marrying off their daughters so young."

"We were lucky with this judge," Nasser said. "Another judge might not have accepted her in court, and would have asked her father or brother to come instead." In all likelihood, Nujood's request would have been denied.

But this judge gave Nujood her divorce. The news of this landmark decision traveled fast, and went global. *Glamour* magazine named her one of their 2008 Women of the Year and she flew to New York City for the celebration. With Shada Nasser by her side, Nujood spoke to the crowd: "Seven months ago, I said the word 'No!' No to child marriage. I hope I've helped many girls like me. I hope to return to Yemen to complete my studies."

"THE STONE THAT DISTURBED THE WATER"

But once Nujood went home, life was still difficult. Despite her fame, a year later the family was living in poverty, and Nujood was an outcast for having been in the spotlight. In 2009, she told CNN, "There's no change since going on TV and speaking to the media."

Then she wrote her memoir, *I Am Nujood, Age 10 and Divorced.* By 2013, her book had been translated into more than a dozen languages, and the publisher had bought a house for her family. For a while, Nujood's earnings paid for her school, but all too soon she stopped benefiting from her success, which was supposed to support her education—and her dream of becoming a lawyer. Instead, she said, her father spent the money. "I've been asked to leave [the house] and have to stay in my older brother's cramped house."

Although things remained difficult for Nujood, her bravery *did* change things— her story inspired other girls to action. Just a few weeks after Nujood's divorce case in 2008, a girl named Arwa managed to get in touch with Shada and asked her to help get a divorce. At eight, Arwa was married to a thirty-five-year-old man, and was treated the same way by her husband that Nujood had been. With Shada's help, Arwa was granted a divorce. Two more cases followed in Yemen. And in nearby Saudi Arabia, a mother of another eight-year-old asked for an annulment for her daughter. After one judge said no twice, a new judge took over and granted the annulment.

On a much larger scale, Nujood's divorce case—and the cases that soon followed—seemed to open the lines of communication. Some people became less fearful of talking about the issues, which sparked a movement to try to change marriage laws in Yemen. "Her case was . . . the stone that disturbed the water," a Yemeni journalist said about Nujood.

In Yemen, the average age of marriage in rural areas is twelve or thirteen, and the country has one of the highest maternal mortality rates in the world. Progress in creating new laws about the appropriate age to marry is slow, as there is much disagreement. For example, in 2011 a member of the Yemeni parliament told *National Geographic* journalist Cynthia Gorney, "If there were any danger in early marriage, Allah would have forbidden it." These beliefs are deeply held. In 2009, parliament voted to make seventeen the minimum age for marriage, but the law didn't pass because some lawmakers felt it was contrary to Islamic law. In 2014, proposals for a new Yemeni constitution included making marriage illegal under the age of eighteen.

Clearly, it is a challenge to change these rules while staying true to the traditions of a culture. Can it be done? Can hope for a better future be realized?

MELKA

FROM ETHIOPIA

"PUT THIS ON, YOU'RE GETTING MARRIED"

Melka, like Yasmin, is another young woman who fought back and attempted to seek justice after surviving a rape. Hers was on her "wedding" night. Melka lives in an Ethiopian village called Libo Kemkem in the northern region of the country. Tall and powerful, with penetrating eyes and a warm smile, Melka sat down with Girl Rising to talk:

"I was fourteen. I had just come home from school and there were so many people at my house. Everyone was dressed up and I asked my mother what was going on, but no one would tell me. More and more people just kept coming. Then my mother brought me a dress and said, 'Here, put this on, you're getting married.' I tried to run, but they beat me. Next to me was a man I had never seen before. I just wanted to get out of there."

But the wedding took place and Melka was sent away with her much older husband. When they arrived at his house, he pushed her toward the bedroom, but she refused. She was beaten again, and her memory became a bit fuzzy after that.

Melka said, "I didn't want to go inside, but no one would listen to me. They just kept pushing. His friends beat me. It's hard to remember, they just kept beating me until I went in. I woke up in the hospital. My whole body was aching. I could barely open my eyes. I couldn't even move. I was there for about thirty days."

The nurses at the hospital reported what had happened to the police. Melka's stepfather, her mother, and the man she had married were all sent to jail. The marriage was annulled. When Melka was ready to leave the hospital, she returned to her home.

But even though the authorities had stepped in to protect Melka, her situation at home was devastating. Her family blamed her for their fate. She said, "When my

After escaping a forced marriage fraught with violence, Melka became a teacher.

parents got out of jail, my father wouldn't even talk to me. I couldn't afford to go back to school, so I had to start working.

"It was hard, but I've come out stronger," Melka said. "Before this happened, I was shy and couldn't even look people in the eye. Now I'm not scared of anything."

"I'M STILL GOING TO GO TO SCHOOL"

Aseya is also from Libo Kemkem, in northern Ethiopia. Melka works at Aseya's school, teaching girls about the dangers of child marriage and about good hygiene and HIV/AIDS prevention.

Aseya was fifteen and in the seventh grade when Richard Robbins met her. Wearing a red shirt and headscarf, Aseya eagerly wrote her name in English for the visitors.

She was confident, and her eyes were bright. Within just a few minutes, she seemed comfortable with her interviewers, and a big grin broke through. When asked her favorite part of the day, she said, "Recess."

Aseya is lucky; in this rural, farming region, she comes from a family that believes in the importance of education. An older brother is a teacher. When asked what she wants to be when she grows up, she said, "A doctor." Richard heard this answer from other Ethiopian girls he interviewed, so he asked Aseya why she thinks so many Ethiopian girls want to be doctors or teachers, or other professions that help people. She told him, "Ethiopia is economically a poor country, so because of that, when we get an education, we don't only need to support ourselves, we have a responsibility to support our family, our parents, our country."

But a year earlier, Aseya's parents had told her something that threatened her dreams. They had arranged for her to be married, and expected her to drop out of school. When she heard this, Aseya went to the Girls' Club at her school to seek help. Members of the female student advisory tried to intervene and told Aseya's parents the marriage should not take place. Her parents were not swayed.

Aseya was not giving up. She told her parents that she really did not want to get married and leave school. Their response? She did not *have* to get married, but she would have to leave the house if she didn't. Aseya knew that leaving home wouldn't have a good outcome at her age, so she proposed a compromise. She asked her parents to put off her marriage for three years, until she turned eighteen, so she could stay home and continue her schooling. Her parents were finally persuaded.

Although the legal age of marriage in Ethiopia was changed to eighteen in 2004, tens of thousands of girls are still married off at fifteen, and some people consider thirteen to be a safe age. Ethiopian girls have also been married as early as seven. *Seven.* That age has been even lower in other countries.

When Richard Robbins heard what Aseya had negotiated with her parents, he asked her what she would do when the three years were up. She said, "I'm going to be married, but I'm still going to go to school." And what if they didn't let her? Aseya tilted her head and raised her eyebrows: "Then I will leave the house." Such strength and tenacity will carry this girl far in life.

"YOU ARE KNOCKING DOWN OUR CULTURE"

Like Aseya, Banchiayehu is an Ethiopian girl who wants to be a doctor. Her favorite subject is physics. When Girl Rising met her, she was sixteen and in the eighth grade. Each day, Banchiayehu walks forty minutes to her school. Unlike Aseya, she is soft-spoken and shy, often covering her mouth when she smiles. But there is a steely indomitability underneath.

Banchiayehu literally ran from a marriage that her father had planned for her in secret—twice. The first time, as family and friends gathered for a celebration at her house, Banchiayehu and her brother Yetsedaw wondered what it was for. They soon realized what their father was up to. Yetsedaw, four years older than Banchiayehu, was in twelfth grade. He knew the laws against marrying under the age of eighteen, and he had seen what life was like for his female cousin and his other sisters. He did not want the same fate for his little sister.

Yetsedaw argued with his father. His father told Yetsedaw that money had already been exchanged, and that this was the way of their people. Yetsedaw did not give in, threatening to call the police and have his own father arrested. Finally, his father backed down, but he was very angry and told him, "You are knocking down our culture." Yetsedaw returned the money to the man's family, and Banchiayehu was relieved and grateful.

Yetsedaw then returned to his school, where he lived in a boys' dorm. But when he came home to visit, he saw that, once again, his family was planning a celebration. At first, it seemed that it was in honor of Easter, but when Yetsedaw saw the family from the first event approaching, he knew his father meant to hide Banchiayehu's marriage ceremony from the police by holding it under the guise of an Easter gathering.

Yetsedaw fought with his father and other family members, telling them he was not going to allow the marriage to take place. When Banchiayehu set off running, her older sister's husband ran after her and dragged her back. Yetsedaw got the police, who stopped the marriage papers from being signed and reminded his family of

Banchiayehu with her brother Yetsedaw.

the law. But after the police left, her family still tried to force Banchiayehu to marry against her will.

Yetsedaw was prepared to fight for her, but so was his family. He took off to get the police again, this time with his father and brother-in-law running after him, trying to hit him with rocks and tie him up. Somehow he stopped them—again. Yetsedaw spent the next few months standing guard over his sister. Finally, the family gave up.

After all this, Yetsedaw believes their parents have had a change of heart. But his neighbors are still angry with him for breaking the ways of their culture. Still, he is glad that his intervention not only saved his sister, but seems to have scared his neighbors enough to stop forcing their daughters to marry.

Banchiayehu is able to stay in school. Her hard work is valued and her poems and drawings are displayed on the outside of their house for all to see. "They are proud of me," Banchiayehu says. "Now they don't want me to get married."

AZMERA

FROM ETHIOPIA

"I GOT MAD AND I TOLD MY TEACHERS"

In another Ethiopian village, another brother came to his sister's aid. Azmera was not yet fourteen when she learned that her mother had agreed for her to marry a twenty-year-old man they had never met before.

Azmera is part of a loving family. She is kindhearted, extremely curious, and painfully shy. Although some of the Ethiopian girls Girl Rising met are assertive and had no trouble speaking their mind, it is more typical for Ethiopian girls, especially in rural areas, to have been taught to avert their eyes or turn their head when they smile. During the research trips Richard Robbins took to Ethiopia, he noted that the majority of the girls he met had this trait in common. He reported, "They do not smile easily, but when they do, it feels like the sun has broken through a bank of heavy clouds."

That sentiment captures Azmera's smile perfectly. Underneath it, there is confidence, a sense of humor, and a healthy dose of stubbornness.

Azmera's family has had its share of loss. Her mother, Etenesh, once had a husband she loved and three children. But her husband died, and then her eldest daughter. Their immediate family is now Etenesh, Azmera, and Azmera's brother, Meselu. Azmera also has her aunts, cousins, and grandmother in the same village. Watching *Girl Rising*'s video outtakes of this family interacting, it is clear how much they love each other as they laugh, and hug, and tell stories.

When their father died, Meselu had to drop out of school. He has been working as a farmer since he was seven or eight. Etenesh, understandably, worried about her daughter's future. Arranging Azmera's marriage seemed to offer Azmera more protection than Etenesh might be able to provide on her own. This is what the elders in her village told Etenesh as well: that marrying off her daughter would be a loving choice for a mother to make.

BROTHERLY LOVE

"Each of our stories pivots on a single
   moment,
That short pause between what is,
And what could be.
In a breath we can decide between what
   we wish to be true,
And what we can make happen."
   —Maaza Mengiste, in *Girl Rising*

Like Yetsedaw, who helped protect and rescue his sister Banchiayehu, Azmera's brother, Meselu, played a big role in Azmera's story. He was working in the fields the day a man came for Azmera's hand in marriage. Meselu went into the house and saw the stranger talking to his mother. He understood what was happening. In "that short pause between what is and what could be," Meselu stepped in.

He said he would sell everything he owned to keep his sister in school, to give her the gift of a life with choices, to give her chances he himself never had. He wanted his sister to get an education, and he knew that if she married, that would never happen. He told their mother Etenesh no.

Meselu's courage ignited Azmera's. She stepped forward and told her mother she wanted a better life. With one bold move, Azmera and Meselu changed the path of Azmera's life forever. Together, they refused the marriage.

Despite growing up with these traditions, Azmera somehow knew this was *not* what was best for her. When her mother told her that a man who wanted to marry her offered her a chance, an opportunity, and that she should go, Azmera said no. She was the first girl in her family to ever do that. Her brother Meselu supported her decision.

Azmera took action. "I got mad and I told my teachers," she later said. Azmera understood—getting married equaled leaving school. This went against her plan to become a doctor.

It was already difficult to fit school into her life because she had so many chores to do at home. This is the reality in many parts of the world. Most girls in rural areas like Azmera's spend a good deal of their time collecting water, chopping firewood, helping with the farming and the cooking, and caring for younger siblings or cousins. Making time for school can only happen after necessary chores are completed. If a girl must leave school to get married, take care of a husband, and start a family, she will probably never find the opportunity to return.

"LET THEM HAVE CHOICES"

Poverty and generations of cultural and religious traditions are complex issues and difficult to change—especially when a large number of people do not agree with the need for change. Yet the consequences of child marriage seem clear. When girls marry young, education ends and the old cycles of poverty, violence, and early childbirth continue.

But a girl who gets an education is able to start a different kind of cycle. She is going to get married later. She is going to have fewer and healthier children. *She* will be healthier. And she is likely to educate her children.

Laws regarding child marriage vary throughout the world. Even properly determining a girl's age is difficult in many places, as birth records are not always kept. But the United Nations (UN) and other organizations are working toward bringing this practice to an end on a global level.

In 2012, the UN created the International Day of the Girl, a worldwide annual event that focuses on girls' equality. Its inaugural event that year was dedicated specifically to the issue of child marriage. And the Commission on the Status of Women (CSW)—a global policy-making body of the UN—has asked for child marriage laws to be reviewed across the world.

Of course, it isn't just the laws that need to change—it's the intentions of the people who live in the countries where child marriage occurs. Local NGO efforts exist in many places to change how people think about child marriage so they will want to follow the laws. One organization, called Girls Not Brides, was founded to bring the smaller NGOs working against child marriage together so their efforts will be more powerful and gain momentum. Today, it is a global partnership of more than 160 NGOs.

Graça Machel, who has been the First Lady of two African nations (Mozambique and South Africa), has fought for human rights her whole life. In 2011, as part of the Elders (a group of independent world leaders working together for peace and human rights), Machel helped found Girls Not Brides. In a BBC interview, reporter Nomsa Maseko asked Machel what effect child marriage has on girls. Machel replied, "It's not only in what you can count. It is mostly in killing inside the sparkle of life. . . . There's much more inside these young girls, these young women, which is, I can say, killed by the practice of child marriage."

Writer Maaza Mengiste talked about her desire for a good ending to Azmera's story:

"My hope for Azmera in the future is that she continues to go to school. That somehow she influences her cousins, her aunts, to bring the young girls in her family into school. To let them have choices the way that she has. And I hope that she continues into high school and college, and no matter what she chooses to do, that one day, if and when she does have a daughter, that she continues the tradition that *she* has started, which is something new."

May her words apply to every girl who needs them.

WORDS TO
LIVE BY

In Nepal, more than seven million people are illiterate. Most of them are female. In 2011, as part of a program they run in ten countries, Room to Read held a writing competition in Nepal. Fifteen-year-old Moni Khan entered, writing a story about recycling to help educate people in an effort to deal with a garbage problem in her city. Moni won the competition, and Room to Read published her book. Moni told Room to Read, "I want to be an author and write more stories."

Around the time she entered the competition, though, Moni suddenly stopped showing up for school. Room to Read discovered that her parents—who were working for pennies a day in a plastics factory to support themselves and their four children—had pulled Moni out of school. "Because of our financial situation," her mother said, "we arranged to have Moni married." She added, "It was not that we did not want Moni to study."

Moni is well aware that being married as a young teen is part of her culture. Both her mother and grandmother married early. But Moni said, "I have seen their sufferings . . . I started to think that child marriage is not an acceptable thing. An education is more important than marriage."

Luckily, Moni's success with writing her story had an enormous impact on her parents. It helped them change their minds about the importance of school. "We will do whatever we can to get her educated," they said. Moni has two sisters, and her accomplishment has paved the way for them to go to school. Moni's parents said, "We will educate all of our daughters now."

Room to Read scholar, Nepal.

La Rinconada, Peru.

LIMITED ACCESS— OR NONE AT ALL

A girl on planet Earth has a one-in-four chance of being born into poverty.

School is not free in more than fifty countries.

In poverty-stricken areas around the world,
schools are scarce and have limited resources.
This school is in Ethiopia.

Imagine a life in which you work as hard as you can every day, from the moment your eyes open until the moment you allow them to close, without being able to improve your family's situation. Yes, there are happy times, laughter, dreams, love, and kindness. But there is barely enough money for food or clothing, and no extra money to pay for educating your children.

This is the picture for so many of our fellow global citizens. As you have learned, in many parts of the world, slavery and child marriage are two major obstacles keeping girls out of school, and poverty is often at the root of those problems.

Poverty limits girls' access to education in other ways, too. Often, there is no school nearby. If there is one, it may not have an adequate building, or schoolbooks, or other supplies. In many places—especially rural or remote locations—there is a shortage of properly trained teachers, or there are none at all. And developing countries struggling with clean water and sanitation issues usually cannot provide any bathrooms in schools, let alone separate facilities for girls. Not having clean or private toilets can keep girls from attending, especially when they are menstruating. "What is the point of giving our children the Right to Education," Indian journalist Kalpana Sharma wrote in the *Hindu,* "if something as basic as toilets are not available in most schools? How can we expect women's literacy rate to improve if young girls feel embarrassed to be in school after puberty because there are no toilets?"

With such limited access to education in so many nations, it is not terribly surprising that, in most of the places Girl Rising visited, the filmmakers met girls who were the first in their families to go to school.

Each girl fought to be there.

A Cambodian girl walks to school through the streets of Phnom Penh.

CHOET

FROM CAMBODIA

HER MOTHER WANTS HER TO QUIT

When Girl Rising visited her school in Cambodia, Choet could not wait for the privacy of a one-on-one interview with the filmmakers. Undaunted, she stood up in the middle of the room packed with seventy-five teenage girls and recounted how her father died when she was five, forcing her and her eight siblings to find work to survive. Choet is the only one in her family who goes to school, and is able to because of a program through Room to Read. She must wake at five a.m. to work in the rice fields, travel eight miles to school and back again, do her evening work in the rice fields, and then complete her homework late at night. She has little to eat and not even enough money to buy a few crackers to quell her hunger.

Despite Choet's determination to be educated, her mother is resentful of the time Choet could be working instead of being in school. Tears dripping from her chin, Choet says, "She doesn't understand. She just tells me, over and over, how my studies mean more work for her in the fields." Her mother wants her to quit. It is a common struggle.

Choet shows her artwork to a Room to Read employee.

SOPATT

FROM CAMBODIA

"A FIRE INSIDE HER"

Girl Rising's Martha Adams met Sopatt when she was seventeen. Sopatt lives in one of the poorest provinces of Cambodia. Her parents are rice farmers. They often have little to eat. They have no electricity or running water. Sopatt has a long walk to and from school, and there are always daily chores to be done. Still, after school, Sopatt rushes home, armed with whatever magazine or newspaper clippings she has been able to scrounge, excited to read to her mother. Unlike Choet's mother, Martha wrote, Sopatt's mother "beamed with pride at their daughter, the student. The reader."

When Martha asked Sopatt to make a wish for *anything* at all in the world, despite all the other things she and her family do not have, Sopatt's one wish was a box of books to read and share with her community. Girl Rising and Room to Read were able to grant that wish.

In Egypt, Girl Rising met Hoda, thirteen, who said she felt "a fire inside her" when watching other children walk to school. At seven, her constant pestering and pleading finally convinced her parents to send her to school. Her success in her studies prompted them to enroll two of their other children. Now Hoda's plans may affect future generations. She says, "When I see my teacher, I want to be in her shoes." Girls like Sopatt and Hoda can be game changers in the mind-sets of their families and communities.

PAYBACK FOR THE CRIME OF WANTING
TO BE EDUCATED

A school may be many miles from a village. Without a car or an extra mule to spare, students must walk. And usually not on paved roads, or places with sidewalks. Girls are trudging up unpaved, muddy mountain roads, through leech-infested waters of rice fields, along stiflingly hot, arid paths to reach their beloved schools. Real dangers await many girls walking alone. Physical attacks, including sexual ones, against girls and women are a common problem.

In many places, violence—and the threat of violence—is directed at girls *because* they go to school. It is a warning, a punishment, a deterrent. The message: if you want to be educated, if you try, there will be a steep price to pay. The headlines in the news confirm this over and over. It happens repeatedly in Somalia when girls are forcibly removed from schools to be given as "wives" to Al-Shabaab fighters. It happened in Pakistan in December 2014 when the Pakistani Taliban killed more than one hundred children at an army school in Peshawar. It happened in Nigeria in April 2014 when a militant Islamic group called Boko Haram (which means "non-Islamic education is a sin") kidnapped three hundred Nigerian schoolgirls. And these are the instances we *hear* about. When two hundred Nigerian girls were rescued from Boko Haram by the Nigerian military in April 2015, it was determined they were *not* from the group of three hundred girls kidnapped a year earlier.

In India, Pakistan, Afghanistan, Jordan, Syria, and many other places, girls have been abducted, sexually abused, poisoned, shot, and had acid thrown on them; their schools have been bombed, burned down, and shut down—all payback for the crime of wanting to be educated. A United Nations report in February 2015 concluded that schools in at least *seventy* countries had been attacked in the prior five years and that the attacks were targeted at girls, parents, and teachers advocating for girls' education. The report noted: "Attacks against girls accessing education persist and, alarmingly, appear in some countries to be occurring with increasing regularity."

Of course, these attacks and threats *do* frighten parents enough to keep their girls at home or take them out of school. In one tiny example of a widespread crisis, after twelve girls were kidnapped from a Somali school by Al-Shabaab, 150 other girls were pulled out by their families. But thankfully, despite these horrific problems, there are many success stories to share.

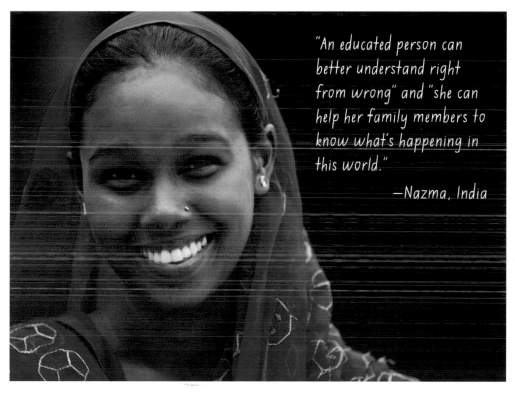

"An educated person can better understand right from wrong" and "she can help her family members to know what's happening in this world."

—Nazma, India

Nazma is the first person in her family to go to school.

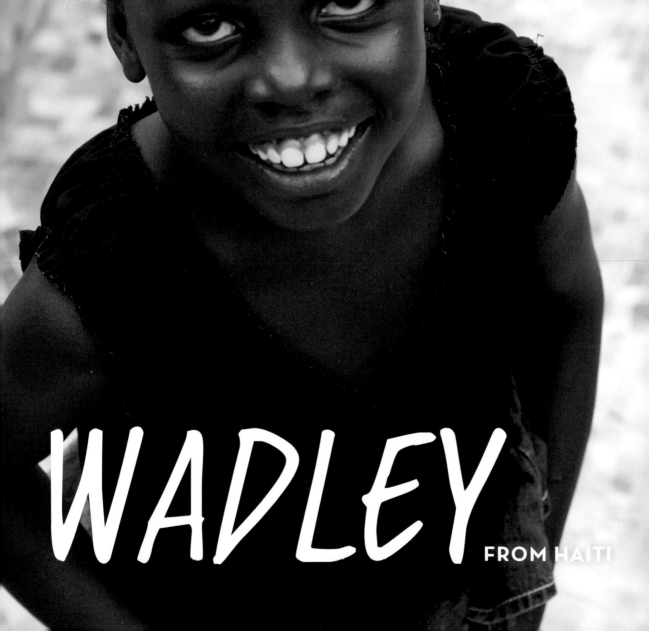

WADLEY

FROM HAITI

SHE MISSED STUDYING AND SEEING HER FRIENDS

Seven-year-old Wadley has a smile that just won't quit. She even smiled when she had to walk through rubble with a bucket to fetch water for her family in the tent camp where they lived after an earthquake wrecked their home in Haiti in 2010. On her trek, she could see her school, also ravaged by the quake. Wadley longed to be sitting at her desk in her school again, studying and seeing her friends. But the earthquake changed everything. Soon, a makeshift school cropped up in the tent camp, but the school cost money, and her family had none to spare. Wadley told Girl Rising she really missed going to school, having homework to do, and learning her lessons. She also missed some of her favorite activities from happier days playing hopscotch or jumping rope with her friends.

Haiti is a little more than seven hundred miles off the coast of Miami, Florida. It occupies about a third of the island of Hispaniola, the rest of which is taken up by its larger neighboring nation, the Dominican Republic. On January 12, 2010, the earthquake that struck Haiti measured 7.0 out of 10 on the Richter scale. Within the next two weeks, there were fifty-two more aftershock quakes. The quakes claimed the lives of more than one hundred thousand people and over a million others were left homeless.

Hundreds of tent camps like the one Wadley lived in were hastily put up—temporary structures of plastic and plywood. With so many people suddenly displaced from their homes into these tent camps, conditions in this small nation rapidly deteriorated. Even before this tragedy, Haiti had severe economic issues that affected many areas of life, including education. There were not enough qualified teachers or supplies, and very little money for public education.

As in many other poverty-stricken nations, paying for school is quite difficult, especially when it comes to finding funds to educate girls. Edwidge Danticat, the

Haitian author who helped Wadley tell her story for the *Girl Rising* film, said: "In Haiti, something like twenty percent of a family's income would be spent sending a child to school. So very poor people, when they have to choose among which of their children to send to school, they will often send the male children. And that's where the girls get left behind. And that's where, I would say, the whole society gets left behind."

Life in the tent camps was dismal. Thousands of people crammed into spaces separated by flimsy dividers, with no sanitation, no security. The situation was often dangerous, especially for women and girls. Sexual violence was common. Since there was often no electricity and little lighting, just walking to a bathroom at night left women and girls vulnerable to attack. Wadley and her family experienced many tense moments in the camp. Luckily, after several weeks, Wadley's family was given a chance to move into a dormitory room at a nearby university that had been transformed into slightly better and safer housing. Although Wadley, her parents, her sister, and all three of her brothers shared one small dorm room, at least they had a door that could be locked, a real roof, and a clean place to sleep.

A DREAMER WHO LOVES TO LAUGH

Despite the challenges Wadley and her family faced, Wadley's radiant smile never faded during the time Edwidge and the Girl Rising team spent with her. For director Richard Robbins, Wadley's attitude was typical of his experience in Haiti. He wrote: "Wandering through a tent camp full of Haitians whose homes were destroyed, I took mental notes: the straight back of a girl carrying a battered plastic jug of water on her head; the steady hand of the man repainting the sign of his makeshift shop; the soothing sound of Creole greetings exchanged between neighbors or friends or strangers; the graffiti which reads *'Tout bagay posib—kwè.'* I asked for a translation. . . . 'Everything is possible—believe.'"

Wadley is a shining example of that mentality, a dreamer who loves to laugh. When she talks about playing with her favorite doll—whom she calls Ashley—

she bursts into giggles. She says her doll never cries and is always happy. Wadley's lightness and optimism made quite an impression on Edwidge. She had a chance to get to know Wadley and talk with her about her life, school, and her dreams for the future. Edwidge, who has a daughter the same age as Wadley, was touched to see how supportive and loving Wadley's family was. She described Wadley as sweet and intelligent, and somewhat dreamy, which reminded her of her own daughter. Wadley yearned to return to school soon, and when Edwidge asked her what she would do if she couldn't go back to school, Wadley told her she would just keep trying until someone said yes.

Edwidge said of Wadley: "She, for me, embodies the hope of Haiti. There is a spark in her that the earthquake didn't destroy, that living in that tent camp didn't destroy, that being out of school for a while didn't take away. She is young enough to be hopeful that she could overcome these obstacles. I find her such a beautiful and magical and hopeful little girl."

Wadley, in Haiti.

SOKHA

FROM CAMBODIA

Another beautiful, magical little girl lived more than ten thousand miles away, in Phnom Penh, Cambodia. But her situation did not seem hopeful. Sokha's home was in a steaming garbage dump teeming with flies, maggots, and mosquitoes. Smoke from burning trash choked the air. The stench was overpowering.

Until 2009, when the Stung Meanchey dump was shut down by the government, this nightmarish scene was the day-in and day-out workplace for a small army of garbage pickers—men, women, and children who lived in shacks at the edge of and on the dump and spent endless hours sifting through hazardous mounds of rotting refuse, rusty nails, broken glass, and discarded needles. They often wore only

The Siem Reap dump in Cambodia, still in use.

flip-flops on their feet; many had no shoes at all. Filth and germs made people sick. When the garbage trucks thundered in to unload more trash, the garbage pickers rushed to rummage through the new piles, while trying to avoid being covered with rubbish as it was dumped—or hit by the trucks. The night shifts were worse, with no light to illuminate dangerous objects, and the trucks kept rolling in.

Nine-year-old Sokha was one of the many children searching for anything of value that might be salvaged and sold. Every step she took through the dump was an opportunity for a sharp edge to cut her, or an ember to burn her. Today, Sokha's legs have the scars to prove it.

In 2008, Sokha was picking through the dump when Bill Smith, an American photographer, learned about her. Bill had been to Cambodia many times, documenting different parts of the country. Six years earlier, in 2002, on a trip with his wife, Lauren, the driver they always used and trusted kept asking Bill if he wanted to see the children. Bill said yes and the driver took them to the Stung Meanchey dump. The visit changed the course of many lives.

"I ALWAYS THOUGHT MY LIFE WAS USELESS"

Bill had already witnessed devastation throughout Cambodia, but nothing had prepared him for the horror of Stung Meanchey. When he and Lauren got back to their hotel that night, they sat in stunned silence, trying to process all they had seen. One photograph in particular he had taken that day—of a little girl in a red hat—haunted him. She was a garbage picker. Bill just kept staring at that picture. He was moved to return to the dump and find her.

He did find her—nine-year-old Srey Na—and met her older sister, Salim, too. With the help of a translator, Bill spoke with the girls' mother and came up with a plan. If she agreed to keep the girls from working in the dump, he would pay their mother the ten to twelve dollars a month they each would have earned working in the dump, and she would send them to a nearby school. The sisters were enrolled in an English-speaking school and attended six days a week.

Back home in Chicago, Bill started rallying his friends to raise money. Soon, they were getting more and more children out of Stung Meanchey and into school. By 2006, with the donations still rolling in, Bill decided it was time to form a proper nonprofit organization. He named it A New Day Cambodia, and it is dedicated to helping house, feed, clothe, and educate as many of the children of the dump as possible. It was only a matter of time before Bill came across Sokha.

Sokha had already suffered many hardships before going to work at the dump. Her mother died when she was little. When her father couldn't find work, Sokha's family lived on the streets for six months. Then her father died, leaving Sokha an orphan. Sokha and one of her sisters took their fate in their own hands. "I had no choice, so I had to decide to work on the dump. It is a bad place," she told CNN in an interview.

"I always thought my life was useless," Sokha said in a video she made about her life. "I had no chance to carry a schoolbag or books to school. Instead, I carried the rubbish bag. . . . Every day I was so hungry, and I picked [from the garbage] some leftover food for my lunch. I worked there for three years." Then one day, Bill Smith returned with his camera.

"I'M A BRAVE GIRL, AND SMART"

Sokha showed up in the photos Bill took that day, and she soon found herself being asked a miraculous question—did she want to go to school? Sokha remembers this time vividly. "When I first arrived at the center, I was a little bit afraid," she told Girl Rising. She soon adjusted, though, and was excited to see all the books at the school. It had a lot of other comforts she had not known before, and Sokha thought the school was a beautiful place. She got in the habit of waking herself up at four-thirty a.m., making her bed, going out in the yard to get some exercise, taking a shower, and then starting to study. Her face lights up when she talks about studying, and, as she says, "I love reading."

Sokha, with *Girl Rising* film writer Loung Ung.

Sokha studied so intently that in 2010 she received a scholarship from Cambodia's Children Education Fund and began attending an excellent school, called Zaman International School. In 2011, Girl Rising learned about Sokha, and paired her with Cambodian writer Loung Ung for the film. Loung was born in Cambodia and grew up there. She now lives in the United States. Loung traveled back to her native home to get to know Sokha and help her tell her story. By the time Loung met her, Sokha had been in school for three years and was totally transformed from her days at the dump. Sokha told Loung what she remembered about the transition:

"When I was young, I was afraid of other people. . . . But right now I'm a brave girl, and smart, and kind. . . . When I first started [school], I went into a room to interview with the principal and I just started with A, B, C. . . . I was so happy . . . it was the first time I could know English."

Sokha was not sure if she would have anything in common with Loung, who travels the world without needing to have a husband or father by her side—a bit of a foreign concept to a typical Cambodian girl. But as they got to know each other,

Sokha and Loung learned that they share important things. They both suffered tragedies in their childhoods and lost their parents at a very early age. Soldiers killed Loung's parents and two sisters during the heinous genocide that took place in Cambodia from 1975 to 1979. Loung and Sokha even told each other they sometimes close their eyes and quietly imagine speaking to their parents to tell them how well they are doing now. As Loung and Sokha talked during their filmed interview sessions for *Girl Rising,* it was easy to see the affection between them when they bumped shoulders accidentally and laughed. They soon discovered another thing they both loved—a good ghost story!

"A CHANCE FOR A BETTER LIFE"

Loung said that Sokha has "nerves of steel. . . . Sokha and I bonded over our outlook on life. . . . I respect her because she is resilient, and graceful, and has a lot of poise." That poise and maturity have served Sokha well. She excelled at school and began to help teach some of the younger students. As time went on, Sokha was teaching English and grammar on Saturdays and Sundays.

Loung sometimes worries that Sokha might feel too much pressure now that she is held up as a role model. "I see the little girls [at school] look up to you. You are like a big sister to them; you're kind to them and you tutor them," Loung said to Sokha. "What do you think they see when they look at you?" Sokha answered, "Maybe they think of why I am smart and why I'm kind, and maybe want to be like me."

Sokha's success and strength of character also made an impression on Richard Robbins. He wrote: "Over the time we were there, it became clear that being such a star also weighs very heavily on Sokha. She has been given something no one else in her family has ever really had—a chance for a better life. . . . Not only has she lived through unspeakable tragedy, but now her great opportunity carries this immense burden. And part of what is so special about this girl is how deeply she seems to understand all this."

Loung asked Sokha what her dream is. Sokha replied, "I want to be a teacher. To open up a school and take in all the students who want to learn." No matter what shape her future takes, Sokha is determined to do everything in her power to accomplish her goals.

Sokha, at school, in her uniform.

SOKHA'S
DANCE

In Cambodia, a traditional form of dance called Aspara dates back to the seventh century, and tells a story. As Sokha describes it, the dance represents a polite, kind, gentle lady who welcomes the foreigner to her country. In the 1950s and '60s, Aspara was performed at the end of the school year to honor the best student. Cambodian girls often begin training for this dance when they are very young so they will have enough flexibility in their wrists and feet to execute the delicate movements flawlessly when they are old enough.

Sokha did not have that opportunity when she was little, but she spent two years learning to dance the Aspara as part of her schooling. She went back to the village where her uncle and other family members lived to perform it for them, and honor the memory of her parents. She also wanted the Girl Rising visitors to see her dance.

In 2011, Sokha was invited to perform the Aspara for the annual Women in the World summit in New York City. First, the audience viewed a short film showing the life Sokha led in the Stung Meanchey dump, and recounting what happened to her after she left. Then Sokha, in the elegant, traditional costume of Aspara, graced the stage. She was transformed in front of their eyes, as her delicate yet powerful dance moved the audience to cheers.

SENNA
FROM PERU

THE POOREST OF THE POOR

Just as Sokha was able to rise out of the smoldering mountain of rubbish in Cambodia, another girl rises from a different mountain—the bleak eighteen-thousand-foot peak of Mount Ananea, in La Rinconada, Peru. La Rinconada, where the thin air makes it hard to breathe, is the highest human habitation in the world. This is Senna's home. Hundreds of years ago, reportedly, this mountain yielded impressive chunks of precious gold. Today, in La Rinconada, the hope that enough gold could be unearthed to make a miner rich caused the population to triple in the past five years, and now eighty thousand people crowd together in this harsh place. Today's miners try to scrape out a living in depleting mines—a huge percentage of which are "informal," which really means illegal—but substantial pieces of gold are rare, and wealth almost impossible to attain. Although Peru's overall national economy is healthy, in La Rinconada it is broken, perhaps beyond repair.

What used to be a beautiful landscape teeming with wildlife has become a destitute area dotted with flimsy tin shacks clinging to the mountainside, water contaminated by sewage and poisonous pollutants from the mining activity and overrun by so much trash that the *Girl Rising* filmmakers decided

La Rinconada, Peru.

to render Senna's story in black-and-white so multicolored piles of garbage didn't visually dominate the scenes. Peruvian-born writer Marie Arana traveled to La Rinconada with Girl Rising and CARE to work with Senna and share her story in the film. This is La Rinconada through Marie's eyes:

"The scrub is gone. The earth is turned. What you see instead, as you approach that distant glacier, is a lunar landscape, pitted with rust-pink lakes that reek of cyanide. . . . The odor is overwhelming; it is the rank stench of the end of things: of burning, of rot, of human excrement. Even the glacial cold, the permafrost, the whipping wind and driving snows cannot mask the smell. As you ascend the mountain, all about you are heaps of garbage, a choking ruin, and sylphlike figures picking idly through it. Closer in are huts of tin and stone, leaning out at seventy-degree angles, and then the ever-present mud, the string of humanity streaming in and out of black holes that scar the cliffs. Along the precipitously winding road, flocks of women in wide skirts scrabble up inclines to scavenge rocks that spill from the mine shafts; the children they don't carry in slings—the ones who are old enough to walk—shoulder bags of rock."

"HE WAS ALWAYS BEHIND US"

Senna, fourteen when Girl Rising first met her, was one of those children. She carried those bags of rock, and she struggled with the weight of many other burdens. In an area where people were already impoverished, Senna and her family were the poorest of the poor. At ten years old, Senna began working in one of the town's two public toilets in the summers and on weekends. She had to clean out the filthy stalls, which stank of urine and feces. When customers came in, she handed them small squares of toilet paper and collected their money, later counting it and giving it to the owner.

This one task of counting offered brief but bright moments for Senna during the drudgery. She loved mathematics and welcomed even this small chance to strengthen her math skills. Her hope of becoming an engineer one day kept her going. To make money, Senna also sold water to people on the street, crushed rock

Senna, with her mother and brother.

from the mines hoping in vain to find any speck of gold, and helped her mother make gelatin treats to sell.

Senna did attend the public school in La Rinconada, but it was difficult to get there, and sometimes she had to miss school in order to work. The price of school supplies and uniforms was also an obstacle. And much of the money Senna earned went to help pay for medicine for her father.

Many years earlier, her father, Juan, had arrived at La Rinconada, strong and healthy, to find his fortune in the mines. There he met Senna's mother. A few years after Senna was born, the shaft Juan was working in collapsed. He escaped but was severely injured. He could no longer be a miner. It was suddenly critical for Juan's whole family to go to work. Juan could cook, though, so five-year-old Senna helped him make things for the rest of the family to sell. As they cooked together in their tiny kitchen, they talked. Senna's father, illiterate himself, understood that educating his children was the only way to save them from a life of poverty. He passed those thoughts on to his daughter.

Juan's health worsened, and he left the mountaintop to seek help. By then, Senna was ten. He never made it back home. Senna desperately wanted to see him again, but transportation was scarce, and by the time her bus reached him, he had died. Senna and her father had always been close, and his absence has left a huge hole in her life. In an interview with *Girl Rising* producer Gina Nemirofsky, Senna said, "He used to give us a lot of love and cherish us, and even though he hadn't gone to school he was able to teach us some mathematics and give us good advice. And he was always behind us, advising us on living a straight-line life."

"IN THE MIDDLE OF A CONVERSATION SHE WILL START SPOUTING POETRY"

That Senna was able to attend school as often as she did was already an accomplishment. In La Rinconada, as the writer Marie Arana explains, "The life of a child is really catch-as-catch-can. There are no laws . . . no one going around to see if children are truant. Nobody cares. . . . The work often takes precedence over education. . . . You're basically trying to survive." Still, Senna longed for a better school, with more qualified teachers and more resources. That required money her family did not have. Senna probably never imagined that her passion for poetry could possibly be the ticket to a better life for her and her family, but that passion made Senna stand out among the other students the *Girl Rising* crew members met in their travels.

As the film crew interviewed Senna, she told many compelling stories. Her pain was almost palpable, her voice cracking, tears spilling down cheeks chapped from constant cold. She described how difficult it is to be ostracized by other students because she is too poor to participate in any extra activities, how her terrible eyesight interferes with being able to see the blackboard or causes double vision when she reads, how devastating losing her beloved father has been. And yet, "In the middle of a conversation," Marie Arana recalled, "she will start spouting poetry. It's the most amazing thing . . . that this child loves something beautiful in such a difficult and hard and punishing place."

Watching Senna break into poetry *is* amazing—much like watching a mesmerizing singer begin a song. It lifts her right out of her chair, and her body moves with the motion of the words, her voice rising and falling with the power of the poetry. Some of the poems are memorizations of other people's work, such as "The Black Heralds," by the great Peruvian poet César Vallejo (which you can hear her recite in the film). Other pieces are her own work. She is a gifted poet, capturing her own experiences and feelings with great heart and skill. And yet poetry is just one facet of this remarkable girl.

"SHE'S GOT A TIGER INSIDE HER"

Even in this harsh environment, Senna has big ideas—not only for herself, but for her community. Gina Nemirofsky asked Senna what she would do differently for La Rinconada if she had the chance to be mayor, and a whole other side of Senna emerged. She began to talk about the devastation of poverty—from the rampant alcohol use to the many brothels in which girls work as prostitutes to make enough money for food. Senna said if she were mayor, "I would concentrate on cantina eradication, alcohol eradication. I wouldn't like to see these girls selling themselves."

When Gina asked her where she hopes to be in twenty years, Senna said, "I see myself in my own business, in my own enterprise. I see myself organizing people, facilitating their work, and after that . . . I would like to just give suggestions and ideas of how houses would be built . . . and if I get that successful, I will help others, too, to make their way easier, not only thinking of myself." One example of how she'd like to help: Senna has ideas about recycling trash in La Rinconada to make it a cleaner, safer place.

Gina also asked Senna if she thought she might return to La Rinconada once she had become an engineer. Senna said, "Yes, I will be back, I will go back and apply all of my knowledge, all of the things I have learned, to try to improve the situations— not the same type of housing, not the same type of transport, or roads, or vehicles." Gina responded: "I think you can do it. They're waiting for you out there." Senna nodded and smiled.

Marie Arana had this to say about Senna: "What struck me most is her absolute profound strength. I don't know where she gets it . . . she's got a tiger inside her." Indeed she does. When asked where she finds her strength, Senna's answer is, "From my family, my heart, and my thoughts." She hopes other girls in similar positions will learn about her experience and "follow" her, as she says, because she is "going to triumph, triumph, triumph."

This medal was a gift to Senna from Girl Rising, in honor of the poetry contests she has won. It says, "For excellence in poetry."

a hope, a dream ...
You, father, who know my sadness, my pain,
you who understand what it is to decay in a lifeless body,
you, who gave me a blazing ray of light,

SENNA'S POETRY

In April 2014, Senna was invited to travel to New York City for the fifth annual Women in the World summit. There, she shared her story, as well as one of her original poems. In honor of her father, Senna recited a piece she wrote in June 2012, entitled "Father."

It was her father who introduced her to writing poems, by asking her to write one for him. His admiration and praise motivated her to continue. She was also inspired by one of her teachers, who had the class memorize poetry with the purpose of reciting it in public. Senna remembers practicing her memorization and recitation skills. She said, "I don't think, that first time, I did appropriate hand movements, but I think maybe by my third time . . . I did very well." She did so well, she won second place in the school competition.

While Senna performed her poem in her native Spanish on the stage at Lincoln Center for Women in the World, the English translation was displayed on a large screen for the audience. Raising her arms to the sky beyond the hall, then kneeling on the ground, her body always in motion with the rhythm of her words, she showed that she is a true artist.

In one of the early interviews Girl Rising did with Senna, Gina Nemirofsky asked her why poetry is so important to her. Senna did not hesitate. "It's a way to reflect on the sad in me." And where does it come from? Gina pressed. "My heart." Here is that poem, straight from Senna's heart.

Senna at Lincoln Center.

Father   Padre

RUKSANA

FROM INDIA

"THE FLOOR IS THE PAVEMENT"

Just as Senna finds solace in her poetry, Ruksana uses paper and pens to transform her sidewalk shelter into a drawing of a beautiful house she imagines living in by a riverbed. Ruksana was ten years old and in the fourth grade when Girl Rising first met her through an organization called World Vision. She and her family had moved to Kolkata, India, from a rural village. They loved their village and were happy there, but there was no work for Ruksana's father, whose dream is to educate his daughters and not marry them off at the age of twelve or thirteen, as can happen. Ruksana's mother was married at thirteen, and had her first child at fourteen.

To attain this dream, they needed to relocate to the city, where he found a job selling sugar cane juice at a market. But he still could not afford a place to live. In Kolkata, Ruksana and her family are known as pavement dwellers. Sooni Taraporevala, the Indian writer who worked with Ruksana to tell her story for the *Girl Rising* film, described their home: "They live on the pavement of a very busy road, which has a tramline running through it. The roof is a tarp and the floor is the pavement, and the wall is another tarp on which they hang their schoolbags." Just steps from the opening to their fifteen-by-seven-foot section of sidewalk, cars zoom by, posing a constant danger. Ruksana's younger siblings have been injured on more than one occasion. They are also vulnerable to crime. And flooding is a real threat, especially during monsoon season. Year-round, the street is a grimy place to live. When Girl Rising's Martha Adams visited Ruksana at home, she wrote this in her field notebook: "Water is a good walk away. Clean water, a myth. Pay-per-use bathrooms are down the block, but the gutter is free."

Pavement dwellers have no legal right to occupy their spot on the street, and the police could evict Ruksana's family at any time. Should that happen to them again—as it has happened in the past—Ruksana's parents told their children to leave everything behind except their school uniforms, shoes, and backpacks. Those are the items they cannot afford to replace.

Keeping their girls safe from the dangers of the street is a real concern that frightens Ruksana's mother. It frightens the girls, too. Ruksana, as well as the other Indian girls Martha and Richard met in Kolkata, revealed that the single greatest fear is the men on the streets at night. To protect her daughters, Ruksana's mother has them walk to a shelter where they can sleep for two rupees a night per girl, plus their help cooking and cleaning at the shelter. But even the walk to the shelter in the dark is precarious. Martha asked Ruksana's mother if she could follow behind the girls one night. As a mother herself, what Martha witnessed terrified her. She wrote, "Hand in hand, Ruskana and two of her sisters walk along crumbling pavement, keeping an eye on mangy dogs, stepping over sleeping rickshaw drivers, past men smoking and playing cards, around mounds of trash. . . . It's dark. This is no place for three young girls. And yet, this is their daily walk to safety."

"ONLY IF THE FILM WILL HELP ALL THE CHILDREN"

Earlier that same evening, Ruksana's mother had invited Martha and the team in for supper. Martha's impressions in her notebook: "Arriving at Ruksana's tarp, we slip off our shoes and step in. It's a steam bath inside and my eyes have to adjust to the dark. Sam, our World Vision representative, our translator Natasha, Ruksana, her siblings, mother, and I all sat down, knees overlapping. . . ." As they shared the lovely meal that Ruksana's mother prepared, Martha thanked her again for allowing Ruksana to represent India in the film. At that moment, Ruksana's mother hesitated for the first time in their conversations about her daughter's participation. She then told Martha it was all right for Ruksana to do it, "but only if the film will help all the children in her community."

Martha was moved by this woman's selflessness. She assured Ruksana's mother that the goal of the film was to help as many girls around the world as possible, both

Ruksana shows drawings she made during her *Girl Rising* interview with Martha Adams.

through building awareness and in partnering with organizations in the local communities where the girls lived to get them the support they needed.

Ruksana told Martha that she loved to draw, so Martha offered her some paper and a pen. Ruksana said she wanted to draw a house, and her picture of a lovely house by the river began to take shape. There was a little boat floating on the river, and fish in the water. Ruksana described the whole picture to Martha. Then Martha asked if she would draw where she lives now. So Ruksana drew a large, modern-looking building with a big tree next to it, and a person standing nearby. But, she said, that wasn't her house; her house was small and next to the building. The translator asked if she could add that to the picture. Ruksana drew a half-moon-shaped plastic roof and a girl lying underneath it, sleeping. As she drew and explained her pictures, Ruksana never once looked sad.

Although Ruksana and her family do not have many possessions, Ruksana has something that is priceless: she comes from a warm, supportive family, and her parents want to ensure a good life for their children. Everything they are doing is for their daughters; every sacrifice is because they understand that educating their children is the best way to give them the tools to create a safe and stable future.

Poverty has taken a terrible toll on this family, but the bonds they share are strong, and they are happy. After spending time in their company, Indian writer Sooni Taraporevala was asked what advice she had for Ruksana. Sooni said, "She is doing so well I have no advice to give her; in fact, I learn from her that you can be happy in whatever circumstances."

Ruksana, in her family's pavement dwelling.

Ruksana, in her school uniform.

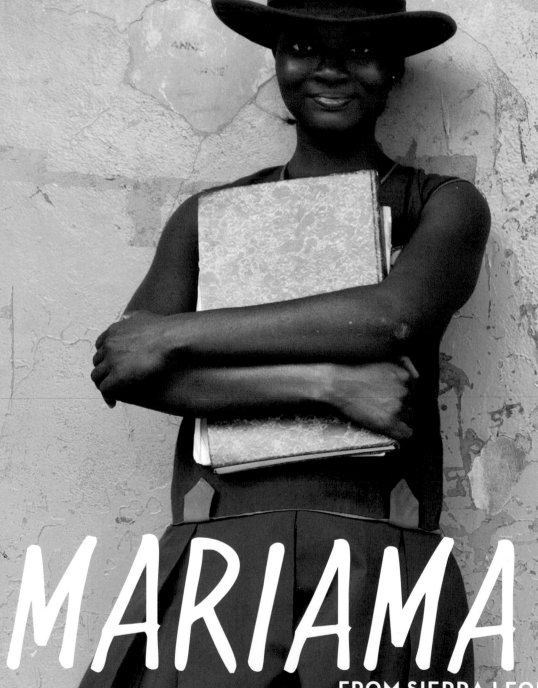

MARIAMA

FROM SIERRA LEONE

THE RESTORATION OF HOPE

Mariama is the first girl in her family to attend school. She lives in Freetown, the capital city of Sierra Leone, on the west coast of Africa. Sierra Leone is home to seventeen ethnic groups, including the Fulani, which is Mariama's heritage. The Fulani was traditionally a nomadic tribe, and one of the first literate groups in West Africa. In the 1990s, the nation tried to reform education and make it more accessible to the general population, but a terrible civil war (1991–2002) broke out. Aminatta Forna is a writer who split her childhood years between two nations—Scotland and Sierra Leone. She said: "The Sierra Leone of my childhood was simply run into the ground by successive corruptive regimes. . . . You were only going to get poorer, and that destroys the soul. It's the lack of hope."

The war made it difficult to create a better educational system. More than 1,200 schools were destroyed and more than 65 percent of children were not being educated. Since the end of the war, a major effort to reopen schools has been under way and enrollment is going up. "Now I'm seeing the restoration of that hope," Aminatta said. Still, there aren't enough schools, or books and other supplies. Qualified teachers are scarce: an estimated 40 percent of primary school teachers are not being properly trained.

The nation also has one of the highest adolescent pregnancy rates in the world, another big factor keeping girls from continuing their education. According to UNICEF, only 15 percent of girls in Sierra Leone make it past primary school to attend secondary school. Despite this fact, Girl Rising had the opportunity to meet several impressive students there.

Mariama is one of them. In many ways, she is a typical teenager—interested in spending her time texting or going out for an ice cream. Aminatta, who worked with Mariama to tell her story for the film, said, "Mariama is so much like a fifteen-year-old girl anywhere in the world, you sometimes wonder if they didn't just all come out of the same factory, at the same time. Her concerns are exactly the same. She asks me whether I think the color of her nail polish she's chosen is the right one for her, and she talks on her cell phone constantly."

"I WAS SO, SO SHY . . . NOWADAYS I WILL TALK TOO MUCH"

An excellent student, Mariama loves science and math. Aminatta said, "We were at the school and Mariama was just sort of working through these formulas. . . . I was dazzled by that. I was absolutely dazzled." Mariama wants to be a doctor or a research scientist, and she is well on her way. And although her mother was not educated, Mariama has other role models all around her now. On a walk through town, Aminatta and Mariama bumped into three women who had graduated from Mariama's school. All three had become doctors. Before they parted, one of them reminded Mariama to never let go of her dreams. It was clear, right there in front of her, that her dream could become a reality.

Mariama and many other girls in Sierra Leone have had a unique opportunity to learn about working at a radio station and talking on the air through a program called Girls Making Media. The program was started by an organization called PLAN West Africa in order to better represent issues that affect girls. Girls Making Media teaches girls how to research, write, and put together radio shows. They are taught how to moderate panels, interview people, and look at all sides of an issue. Topics the girls often tackle include furthering girls' education, teen pregnancy, violence against women, and gender discrimination. The shows are broadcast throughout Sierra Leone, where radio is a big part of the culture. Aminatta explained, "In the postwar years, radio played a phenomenal role in raising awareness, motivating people, helping in the reconstruction efforts in this country. . . . Everywhere you go you see people listening to their transistor radio . . . so quite quickly, Sierra Leonians began to see the potential of radio and really using it to start to debate some of the problems the country was having."

Using it as a focus for girls to reach out to others was a stroke of genius. One of the things Mariama enjoys about her radio show is being able to connect with teenage girls who call in with a problem and give them her advice. "It's something that she obviously loves," Aminatta said, "almost as much as she loves maths, physics, biology, and chemistry. And she feels—and I think she's absolutely right—that she's contributing a terrific amount."

Other girls who have participated in the Girls Making Media program say that it has transformed them from shy to confident, unafraid to speak out, and truly interested in advising and advocating for girls. They believe what they are doing is very important because it is sensitizing both boys and girls to these important issues. During one of her interviews with Girl Rising, Mariama was asked how being on the radio had changed her. Mariama and the translator started laughing, as Mariama explained, "I was so, so shy . . . it wasn't easy for me to talk, and nowadays I will talk too much."

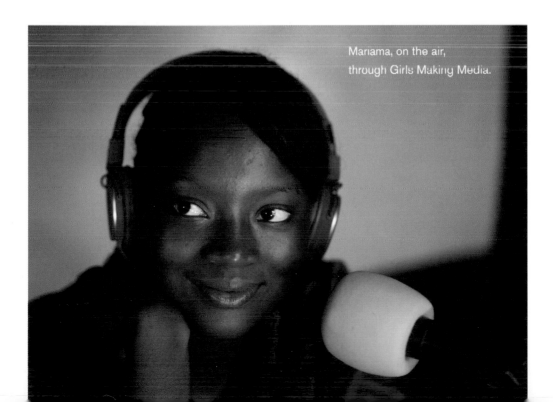

Mariama, on the air, through Girls Making Media.

M'BALLU

FROM SIERRA LEONE

MY DAUGHTER WILL GO TO SCHOOL, TOO

Sixteen-year-old M'ballu has also been changed by working on the radio through Girls Making Media. Not only did she learn to speak out, she noticed a real shift in how adults valued what she and the other girls in the program had to say. "At first, when a child wants to talk," she said, "they would say 'you are very small,' even in decision making, they would say 'your idea has not yet matured.'" But then her mother began to ask M'ballu her opinion and to take her seriously.

M'ballu is a funny, upbeat girl who loves to tell stories and read. Her English is excellent. Her father died when she was very young, and she now lives with her mother—who was never schooled—as well as two brothers and a sister. All four children are in school, and they do everything they can to find a way to pay. "The little that she has," M'ballu says about her mother, "she will give to me."

When M'ballu was small, she used to love pretending to be a lawyer and trying to settle disputes. She hates it when people try to take rights away from others. This attitude may play a role in her career at some point—and it already has in her work on the radio. She now understands the impact the media can have. "When I go on the radio, the whole community can hear it. But saying it to my friends, only my friends will hear it. It's important. . . . Things are changing," she said. "Girls have rights as well as boys."

M'ballu understands the power of education and how it can affect her future. Some of her peers have gotten married, but she does not want that for herself. "If I go to school, my life will improve more than if I marry. . . . I don't want to be in the bush selling palm wine. . . . I would just like to be in my office, possibly doing my office work. I don't want to be in the bush . . . like my mother."

She says that because her mother isn't educated, she now looks to M'ballu for advice. But should she have a daughter, she says, "My daughter will have to go to school, too."

PRICILLA

FROM SIERRA LEONE

"EDUCATION IS BETTER THAN SILVER AND GOLD"

At just twelve years old, Pricilla, another girl from Sierra Leone, has a deep understanding of the importance of school that is far beyond her years. And with good reason. "Most of my lifetime, I spent much time on the streets," Pricilla said. Her mother is uneducated and her father is mentally unstable, so she had to work in the markets to help earn money for her family. The one thing she looked forward to was seeing her friends, but one by one, she said, "they abandoned me because I was so poor."

Now that she is able to go to school (through the help of a local NGO), she is much happier, and has found friends again. Pricilla says she is "the champion" at a dancing game in which patterns have to be copied and repeated. She is generally good at athletics, and her favorite sport is volleyball. "I like to serve the ball, and I like to be with the team." Her favorite subjects are math and English, and she really enjoys Shakespeare; she recounted the complex story of *The Merchant of Venice* for her interviewers. "I like that book," she said, "because it shows you how to judge if somebody is right or wrong." Pricilla's intelligence and maturity are easy to see; what is difficult is to imagine the life she led before she was able to attend school.

When Girl Rising's Beth Osisek asked Pricilla what she would wish for if she had one wish, Pricilla said, "I wish that when I am educated, I could do nursing. . . . I like nursing. They cure people, they save lives. I want to do the same thing, to save people." Pricilla is poised to do great things if she is able to continue her education. Gina Nemirofsky asked Pricilla: if she could meet the president of Sierra Leone and ask him to change one thing, what would she change? Pricilla said, "I want him to strengthen education. Education is better than silver and gold." At twelve, Pricilla already has words of wisdom for us all. "We all are the same," she said. "We both have arms and legs. Regardless of the money that you have, if I am poor and you are rich, let us walk together."

DADS EMPOWERING DAUGHTERS

Shabana Basij-Rasikh (read more of her story in part 3) is the cofounder and president of SOLA—School of Leadership, Afghanistan. It is the first boarding school for Afghan girls. For Shabana, her maternal grandfather—who chose to educate his daughter, Shabana's mother—and her father, who was the first in his family to go to school, sparked her journey. Shabana's father never questioned that he would educate his daughters, despite the risk from the Taliban, which had made school for girls illegal in 1996. When Shabana was scared or uncertain, he told her, "You can lose everything you own in your life ... but the one thing that will always remain in you is what is here [pointing to the brain]."

Although the Taliban is no longer in charge of the government, threats to those who openly educate girls are still present. But Shabana witnesses the same daily support and passion in the fathers of her SOLA students that her father showed her. It is important to acknowledge the tremendous impact men have on the advancement of girls all over the world. And in Afghanistan, Shabana says, "Behind every successful woman, there is always a father who recognized the value in his daughter."

In a place where educating girls is often considered foolish, as daughters may then leave the home to live and work elsewhere, these fathers understand the positive aspects of that. As one SOLA student's father said, "My effort to educate [my daughter] is not a waste because if she won't directly benefit me, at least she would be able to take care of her family and I wouldn't have to worry about her."

Shabana has seen this wisdom and dedication of fathers many times over—in the student who did not immediately get accepted to SOLA, but showed up at the school to request an interview anyway—her father by her side. Or in the student whose father received direct threats to stop sending his daughter to SOLA, but continued anyway. That girl said, "If my father can stand up to threats for me, so should I stand up for my rights and my father's confidence in me." And Shabana has also seen it in Uzma, a former SOLA student who earned a scholarship to a private school in the United States. Uzma said, "My parents are my role models, especially my father. . . . My father has said, 'We named you Uzma, which means *grand,* and we expect you to bring grand changes to the world with your education.'"

Despite the obstacles, girls around the world are able to persevere and get an education. Throughout his travels for the film, Richard Robbins was astounded by these girls. One day, he wrote in his notebook: "I think we are always looking for some explanation of how they can be so tenacious, so determined. 'Was there someone in your life who always believed in you?' Often, no. 'How did you know that you deserved more than what you had?' 'I just felt it inside me.' 'What did you tell yourself in your hardest days so that you would not give up?' 'I told myself not to give up.' And we just keep wondering where the magic in them comes from . . . we are left to marvel at the human spirit. It simply finds a way, when no way exists."

Hope Village teaches survival skills to street children in Cairo, Egypt.
The students in this all-girls karate class say it makes them feel safer and more powerful.

PART THREE

THE SOLUTIONS—
CAN WE CHANGE THE WORLD?

"You don't have to be thirty to start an initiative. You can be as young as you can be . . . you just have to have the drive to do so and the will to do so. Anything can happen once you put your mind to it."

—HANNAH GODEFA,
UNICEF AMBASSADOR AT AGE FIFTEEN

HOW CAN WE CHANGE THE FUTURE?

One of the highlights of researching and writing a book like this is the sense of hope that comes from discovering the variety of people who dedicate their time to solving problems for others. Some end up making it their life's work with an NGO or other organization; others are simply individuals who, in their travels, come across a problem and are inspired to take action to find a way to do something about it. Creative ideas—and people implementing them—are everywhere. Maybe one of these stories will spark an idea for you.

In Cambodia, just a few months before the Stung Meanchey dump Sokha had lived in was shut down for good, an Australian woman named Amy Hanson saw people scavenging in bare feet or flimsy footwear. She promptly started the Small Steps Project. Through her project, Amy delivered hundreds of pairs of boots—as well as other supplies such as water and food—to the people there.

In Afghanistan, Shabana Basij-Rasikh is tackling education for girls head-on. She was born and raised in Kabul. When she was six, the Taliban made it illegal for Afghan girls to attend school. Despite the dangers, Shabana's parents encouraged her and her sister to go, even though the only option was to walk forty-five minutes each way to a secret school in the living room of a woman no longer allowed to be a high school principal. Each day, more than one hundred girls would make their way to her house, taking different routes each time to avoid being followed, staggering their arrival and departure times, pretending to be various family members coming and going.

When the Taliban regime collapsed in 2002, the joy in Shabana's household was palpable. Her father said, "You can go to a *real* school now. You don't have to go to that secret school anymore." It was a moment Shabana will never forget. Shabana later spent her senior year in high school in Wisconsin, through an exchange program funded by the U.S. State Department, before attending Middlebury College, in Vermont.

At Middlebury, Shabana reflected on her educational background with deep gratitude. "People usually appreciate something when they are denied it. In my case it was education, and I have never gone a day without giving thanks for the opportunities I was given," she said in an interview. She was moved to do something to help girls back in Afghanistan. Since the collapse of the Taliban, the situation for women has improved, but as you now know, girls still take serious risks by going to school. In 2008, while still in college halfway across the world, Shabana cofounded SOLA—School of Leadership, Afghanistan. It is Afghanistan's first boarding school for girls ages twelve to eighteen. The ripple effect is happening quickly through SOLA—graduates are moving on to study at universities, as well as embark on meaningful careers.

Shabana Basij-Rasikh (right), with SOLA scholar Uzma (left), at a gender-equality event in New York City, March 2015.

Even seemingly small practices can make a big difference. For example, in countries such as Brazil, Mexico, Bangladesh, Turkey, Nigeria, and others, cash transfer programs are offered to families to send girls to school. The ways in which these programs operate vary, but they function on the basic idea that if a family is given enough financial support they won't have to resort to keeping daughters home to work. These programs have had a positive impact on increasing girls' enrollment in schools worldwide. An overwhelming number of innovative practices are being dreamed up and put into action by people, organizations, and governments all over the world.

A COMIC BOOK TACKLES A TABOO

In India and other parts of the world, there is a shame associated with menstruation. Girls are often kept at home during this time, and have many other social restrictions as well—they may not be allowed to sit on family furniture, attend their place of worship, eat at the dinner table, or go to school. A large part of this problem is that there is often no education about menstruation, so it is considered taboo, something to be ashamed of and kept hidden.

A young Indian woman named Aditi Gupta wanted to do something about this. In March 2013, she and her college friend Tuhin Paul began to cocreate a comic book called *Menstrupedia* to teach Indian girls about their periods. They wanted to make the material accessible in a fun way so people wouldn't be ashamed to read about menstruation. Their prototype caught on quickly, and boys, who were in the dark as much as girls, wanted to read it, too.

Their path to completion was fairly quick. Aditi and Tuhin wrote a script, raised money through crowd funding, and continued working on storyboards and illustrations. By April 2014, the first chapter was up on their website as a free download, and by September, the comic book was ready to ship! Aditi and Tuhin consider their efforts to be a small change, but small changes lead to big ones, and the educational impact of their comic book is likely to have the critical result of more Indian girls remaining in school during their periods. In fact, *Menstrupedia* has already been used to educate 24,000 girls across India, and has been translated into seven languages, including Nepali and Spanish.

WHAT CAN YOU DO?

Are you fired up? Do you want to create change in the world? You can! There are lots of things you can do to make an impact. Start with your own voice. As you've seen, so many girls' voices around the world are squelched; they are not heard. Speak out for those who can't. Write an op-ed piece for your school or community newspaper and share some of the things you have learned. Even something that may seem as insignificant as posting information on social media about some of these issues can make a big difference in raising awareness. Getting people talking leads to generating ideas, which leads to things happening. As these issues become a regular part of our conversations, momentum grows.

Another seemingly small act that has a far-reaching impact is purchasing foods and other products with the Fair Trade certification symbol. Fair Trade nonprofits work with farmers around the world—often in impoverished countries—to guarantee that they are paid fair wages, have safe working conditions, and are not hurting the environment with their farming practices. Fair Trade partners earn development funds to use where they are most needed in their local communities for anything from health care and nutrition to literacy and access to education. In many places, these partnerships help to keep kids in school because when farmers are making a fair wage, they are less likely to need their children to stay home and work.

The effects are felt well beyond the farming families themselves. In Ghana, schools have been built with Fair Trade profits. In Paraguay, Fair Trade funds from sales of sugar provide computers, books, uniforms, and other school supplies. In India, the money has gone to buy buses to transport students from remote villages to their schools. The examples go on and on, and all stem from supporting a system of fair trade that helps in the global fight against poverty.

USE WHAT YOU LOVE TO INSPIRE CHANGE

Do you love to cycle, or sing, or write? Are you into fashion, theater, art, or basketball? No matter what your particular passion, you can channel it into a project to effect change and have a blast in the process. Put together a fashion show, a poetry slam, a hoops competition, or a cabaret and raise money for one of the nonprofit organizations you have learned about—or research a new one to support. In Tajikistan, a Youth Theater Peace Program develops and performs plays about issues that mirror its participants' own lives—child marriage, girls' education, and changing gender roles. In Senegal, a group of teenagers made a video about forced marriage that sparked such interest they turned it into a feature film. Their storytelling skills made a huge impact.

If you have visual art talent, you could raise awareness by creating public art for some of the data included in this book. Find an interesting or innovative way to transform any of the statistics or graphs into original works of art. How many different ways can you imagine visually representing the ripple effect described in part 1, for example? You could display this work locally at your school. You might even want to get a few other like-minded artists together and create an exhibit or art show and invite the public. Get people talking! Your artistic reach could be even wider depending on how you choose to share your artwork. Maybe you want to shoot a video of what you've created and upload it to a blog or other website, or let the local media know about it.

If you are an avid bicyclist, you may be interested to know there are several organizations delivering bikes to people in developing nations who cannot afford transportation to get to work or school. World Bicycle Relief is the largest group, having already gotten fifty thousand bikes to people in remote areas of Africa. Another group is called Wheels 4 Life, and it has delivered more than seven thousand bikes to people in Kenya, Madagascar, Tanzania, Costa Rica, Uganda, and many other countries. The organization generally tries to buy the bikes in the same countries where they donate

Students sharing a bike to their Room to Read school in rural Cambodia.

them, to keep the business local as well. To keep costs down, most of the people who work for Wheels 4 Life volunteer their time. And in 2010, inspired by Martha Adams's work in Cambodia with Girl Rising, Kevin and Clare Cohen founded Pink Bike. Together, Girl Rising and Pink Bike have gotten bikes to hundreds of girls in Cambodia, Sudan, and Nepal. You can support any of these groups by directly making a donation, or organizing your own fund-raiser.

Are you a writer? You could write a guest blog post as a youth contributor for the Elders, a global website of world leaders such as Mary Robinson, Desmond Tutu, and Graça Machel who have joined forces to tackle human rights issues like equality and education for girls and women. You could choose which issue in this book elicited the strongest response in you and write your thoughts on it for your school paper, watch the *Girl Rising* film and write a review, or write your own screenplay, short story, essay, or poem and share it with your community.

To support the efforts of teen writers struggling to find their voices, you could make an online visit to the Afghan Women's Writing Project (AWWP) Teenage Writers Workshop and start a "commenting campaign." The workshop offers Afghan girls transportation, time, and Internet service at an Internet café in Kabul so they can learn how to tell their stories in English, and therefore have their stories more widely shared. The AWWP's website publishes the girls' essays, stories, and poetry, and constructive or supportive comments will help these girls feel heard.

DESMOND TUTU'S MESSAGE TO MEN AND BOYS

Archbishop Desmond Tutu is a founding member of the Elders, a unique group of male and female peacemakers brought together by the late Nelson Mandela in 2007. Elders no longer hold any political office, so they are not beholden to any government. Instead, they bring their lifelong expertise and passion for pioneering change to this extraordinary group. I think of them as our wisest grandparents, dedicating themselves to the good of our global village.

On the topics of child marriage and equal rights for girls and women, Tutu recognizes the need for men to be as involved in creating change as women. He explained the reality in many parts of the world: "Child marriage occurs because we men allow it. Fathers, village chiefs, religious leaders, decision-makers—most are male. In order for this harmful practice to end, we need to enlist the support of all the men who know this is wrong, and work together to persuade all those who don't."

In an open letter on the Elders website, Tutu delivered this message: "I want to encourage boys to stand up for their sisters, and say that girls have the same rights to go to school, to develop and be everything they can be. . . . We men have to be bold, to speak the truth and stand up for the rights of girls and women to equality, dignity, and the rights we all share."

Desmond Tutu.

BE A WARRIOR

The words "warrior" and "revolutionary" have come up in the context of girls who have fought their way to a better future. You can be a warrior, too—on behalf of any girl who needs someone to stand with her. There are exciting volunteer opportunities with organizations like Girl Up. Girl Up is the United Nations Foundation's adolescent girl campaign, which empowers people to become advocates for girls' issues worldwide. Their website has a lot of information about advocacy—reaching out to your elected officials to take action on a given cause. And Girl Up is equipped to help you contact your local representatives by phone or in writing. If you want to schedule an in-person meeting, Girl Up can show you how to do that, too. Girls between the ages of thirteen and eighteen are eligible to become Teen Advisors for Girl Up. Visit the Girl Up website to learn more about that opportunity.

Girl Rising has a program enabling teenagers to take a leadership role in the global movement for girls' education. Girl Rising Ambassadors represent Girl Rising in their communities—you might host a screening, brainstorm ways to raise awareness, or work with the Girl Rising team to connect global efforts to your community. Each Ambassador also plans at least one event for the annual global International Day of the Girl in October. More information and an Ambassador application are available on the Girl Rising website.

Perhaps you have your own idea for a nonprofit and are passionate enough to start one. Many organizations are begun from just that—a great idea, and the motivation to work at it. One step at a time, you can accomplish anything!

Hannah Godefa is a great example of this. She is a teenager from Toronto. In 2005, when she was seven, she visited her parents' hometown in rural Ethiopia. It was her first time in Ethiopia, and she was excited to stay with her grandmother and see what life was like there. During her trip, she made a close friend. Hannah wanted to stay in touch as pen pals, but her Ethiopian friend had no paper or pencils. Hannah learned that this was a widespread problem.

Just like that, Hannah saw a need and wanted to meet it. In a television interview in 2011, she said, "I really had a vision to eliminate any barrier of education through school resources. . . . I wanted to solve this . . . lack of resources for all Ethiopian children." This is exactly how amazing projects can start, but persistence is paramount for success. Back home, Hannah proposed her idea to her school principal. "At first, he really didn't believe in my idea. But I kept on going back again and again . . . finally he saw that I was serious about my vision." From there, she reached out to her community and spoke to the media, and began collecting pencils. She called her project Pencil Mountain.

Young people may sometimes feel as though their voices don't matter to adults, or that they aren't taken seriously. But Hannah quickly saw that the opposite is often true. Determination and vision in young people is admired and respected. The media took notice, and news of Pencil Mountain spread. People volunteered to help. In 2006, Hannah returned to Ethiopia to deliver about twenty-five thousand pencils. By 2012, that number had climbed to half a million.

When in Ethiopia in 2006, Hannah had another chance to learn about village life. She was shocked to discover how common it is for girls to be kept out of school to do household work, while boys are sent to school. This knowledge motivated her and fueled her imagination. Since that time, she has put many ideas into action, collecting research books for Ethiopian universities, getting wheelchairs to disabled students, and speaking out around the world about the right to education.

In 2013, at age fifteen, Hannah became a UNICEF National Ambassador to Ethiopia. And it all began with a seven-year-old's desire to help. Hannah said, "I have a social responsibility to help children in Ethiopia. And because I've had the insight that I did in Canada, and because I had the opportunity to get an education, that's my motivation to want to provide the same opportunity to children here in Ethiopia."

While Hannah *is* remarkable, nothing she did was beyond reach. She would likely agree that anyone with determination could accomplish similar goals. Including you. Especially you. The idea of trying to save the world is daunting. But small changes can make a big difference, especially when you join forces with others.

Hannah Godefa volunteering for the Child to Child Programme through UNICEF Ethiopia.

Azmera, Ethiopia.

GIRLS RISING

Education = The Power of Possibility

As we just saw, our individual efforts have the power to make a major impact on the world around us. This holds true for the girls you have met here, too. Of course, not every story has a clear-cut ending, and there is no foolproof fix for some of the larger issues we've encountered. But most of the girls (as well as some siblings and family members) receiving financial support through Girl Rising are doing quite well. They have been able to rise up and out of their circumstances. How is their newfound education impacting their lives—and how might it, in turn, enable *them* to change the world? Let's find out how some of the girls are not only forging their own paths, but in so doing are preparing to help others someday.

Sokha (and Srey Na) meet Michelle Obama at the White House.

SOKHA, CAMBODIA

From July to August 2014, Sokha was enrolled in a summer leadership academy through the Council on International Educational Exchange (CIEE). She traveled from Cambodia to Dakar, Senegal, in West Africa, where she worked with other peer leaders, and was exposed to different studies, such as photography and sustainable forestry. On one of their field trips, she saw the desert and rode on a camel. Through social media, Sokha chatted with me about that trip, saying, "That was awesome and fresh, even if it was so hot." Part of the program included service projects as well, and Sokha volunteered in an orphanage. She spent time with the children there, taking them outside to play, and getting to know them. Learning to speak some of the languages by taking CIEE's "survival language class" was another important piece of this educational exchange. "The languages were Wolof and French," she shared, and "I enjoyed learning them. I could communicate with people, which made me so joyful."

In March 2015, Sokha had another incredible opportunity, closer to home. She had met First Lady Michelle Obama while visiting the United States a few years earlier. Sokha introduced herself as "a child of the dump" and invited the First Lady to visit her homeland. So when Michelle Obama went to Cambodia in 2015 to talk about the Let Girls Learn initiative that she and President Barack Obama had launched, she invited Sokha to join her at a school visit in the Siem Reap province. The mission of Let Girls Learn is to support community efforts globally to get girls in schools and keep them there—something Sokha cares about deeply. Peace Corps volunteers will run the programs, and Cambodia—where only about 20 percent of children finish secondary school—is one of the initial eleven countries that will benefit from the initiative.

Not only was Sokha invited to attend, but she actually had a chance to talk about education with Michelle Obama, as well as Cambodia's First Lady, Bun Rany, when both women visited with students. Sokha was included in further conversations with Michelle Obama as part of a small roundtable discussion with some of the Peace Corps volunteers—and she was seated beside the First Lady. Their discussion focused on supporting girls' education in Cambodia. Sokha said, "It was wonderful . . . marvelous . . . we shared ideas and found ways to solve [problems] together."

Sokha also told me about some business classes she was taking in April 2015 and that she had gotten interested in studying how to manage a business or organization. Finishing her education is her main focus: in 2016 she reached the twelfth grade and was enjoying a full schedule of classes. Her enthusiasm for learning had not waned one tiny bit. "I love reading books during my free time." Not that she has a lot of it—she takes extra classes on weekends and plans to apply to college in the United States.

Sita with her mother.

SITA, NEPAL

Although Sita endured being a *kamlari* for four years, once she was liberated and back at school, she began to speak out against the *kamlari* practice with the Nepal Youth Foundation (NYF). Sita's education serves her well. She has a wonderful ability to clearly express her viewpoint. Her bold voice even saved her sister from being sold into *kamlari*. And she helped her mother learn how to write her name.

SUMA, NEPAL

Unlike Sita, Suma did not have any schooling prior to her many years as a *kamlari* and is still making up for lost time. This is very common—and understandable—among former *kamlari* girls. She did not pass the national exams to move on to grade ten, but did complete a twenty-nine-month program the NYF offers to become a community medical assistant. She is taking courses in computer skills and the English language. Suma is quite active as a peer counselor for the NYF and involved in a cooperative the NYF established to assist former *kamlari* girls.

Suma wants to open a medical clinic in her village and is dedicated to continuing to protect the rights of girls. She now has the tools to make that happen.

SENNA, PERU

In June 2013, Senna and her family were relocated off the mountain, and she and her brother Henry were both enrolled in a better school. Senna told Girl Rising, "My life has changed a lot. I came here, I saw new things. . . . I like my school very much. I feel comfortable with my classmates."

In her new house, instead of the whole family living cramped in a small space together, Senna got her own bedroom, where she can study. She also received her first pair of eyeglasses, which made a huge difference in her ability to study and see the blackboard at school. Senna graduated from secondary school on December 27, 2013. She wore a fancy dress, heels, and makeup, and looked quite different from the girl the film crew had first met in La Rinconada. Senna said, "I feel happy about the future, because I know I'll be a professional. I will study hard so I can make it into the university."

In January 2014, she achieved that goal and began studying business. That same year, in June, Senna was in Lima for a conference about women's education. And that December, Senna was profiled in a feature on Peru's "anonymous heroes" in the Peruvian magazine *Somos*. In the video footage and photographs of Senna with her university friends and in her new home, joking with Henry, making faces at the camera, it was apparent that some of the sadness that shadowed her face when she lived on the mountain has dissipated, and she is on her way to turning the life she imagines into a reality.

Of course, many people stumble under the best of circumstances, and Senna has had significant hardships along the way. But she has always known she has a challenging road ahead of her that will require determination. When Girl Rising first met Senna at fourteen, Gina Nemirofsky asked her about her dreams of becoming an engineer and whether she foresaw any obstacles in her path. Senna said, "I think it's not going to be easy at all. Perhaps I will have some problems. . . . It's going to take time." She did struggle with some of her grades, and Senna sometimes finds it difficult to move past painful memories. She also feels the pressure to succeed at the goals she has set for herself, and to live up to the scholarships and opportunities she has been given.

One more huge change affecting her life is that Senna had a baby in September 2015. She was eighteen then, and her mother—as well as the baby's father—planned to help her care for the baby. Senna was more determined than ever to finish her schooling so she could provide a better future for her child. Senna also intends to keep writing poetry. It's clear that Senna's sheer drive and passion to succeed will serve her well in whatever she does.

MARIAMA, SIERRA LEONE

Mariama and her family are well. She has developed a strong interest in science, and her teachers say she is very studious. At school, she is active in the debate society and drama, and acts as the organizing secretary of the drama club. With the support she is getting, Mariama is able to focus so well on her studies that in 2016 she took the required entrance exams so she could apply to university. She passed on her first attempt!

RUKSANA, INDIA

As of this writing, Ruksana and her family were still living in their shelter on the pavement in Kolkata, and she and her three sisters continued to sleep at the night shelter near their home. All of her siblings were enrolled in school, and her father was running his own sugar cane juice trolley, which was a gift from the Girl Rising production company. That summer, Ruksana also joined the Girl Rising team in Delhi to help launch Girl Rising India, which included a new Bollywood version of the film in Hindi.

Earlier that year, Ruksana participated in World Vision's Life Skills for Transformational Development (LSTD) Program. The five-day program uses songs, dances, skits, and other activities to teach kids about child rights, health, nutrition, and the importance of education.

Ruksana was attending Metropolitan Girls High School as well, and was an exemplary student. Alongside her academics, she studied dance, karate, and drawing. Her artwork is important to her, and she wants to be an art teacher in her community when she is older. Girl Rising began funding additional English language classes for Ruksana, her siblings, and other girls in her community.

MELKA, ETHIOPIA

Although Melka went through a horrific experience on the night of her forced marriage, her intelligence and her will were undiminished. She became a teacher. Melka said about teaching, "No one asked me to do this work. I do it because I have to and because, when I was growing up, everyone said it was unlucky to have a daughter, to be a girl. I didn't believe that. . . . In my village, girls have to work hard, we don't have that much. But we still dream

of becoming doctors and teachers. I'm doing this because I can't let what happened to me happen to anyone else. . . . Here at the school, I teach girls about their rights. I do this so that other girls don't have to go through what I went through. I want them to know that it's not unlucky to be a girl in Ethiopia."

AZMERA, ETHIOPIA

Azmera was also thriving when we checked in with her in May 2015. She and her mother, Etenesh, were living together, and Etenesh was supportive of Azmera's studies. Azmera was number six in the ranking of the forty-five students at her school, and was striving to become number one! Etenesh was farming their land in cooperation with Azmera's uncle, which increased their income and made home life more stable.

WADLEY, HAITI

Wadley has been busy! In November 2013, she had a chance to meet with U.S. secretary of education Arne Duncan when he visited Port-au-Prince for an education conference. Duncan was in Haiti to announce a grant to provide more access to education in Haiti. Wadley, known by then for her role in *Girl Rising*, was invited to attend that meeting. Cate Oswald, who works for Partners in Health (PIH), which helped support Wadley and her family after the earthquake, has got-

ten to know Wadley pretty well since that time. Oswald went with Wadley to meet Duncan and to translate for her.

"It was really sweet to see how the major education policy leaders of the U.S. were starstruck meeting Wadley and all wanted pictures with her," Oswald said.

"They've all seen the movie *Girl Rising* and are huge fans of Wadley and her perseverance that kept her in school."

Because of that, Duncan was quite interested in hearing Wadley's thoughts. She wasted no time telling him that Haiti needed more books, better Internet, and lots of trained teachers. When she told Duncan how much she loved math, the two engaged in a challenge of solving mathematical problems.

In January 2015—five years after the earthquake devastated her home—Wadley turned twelve. By that time, the picture of her world was looking much different. She was attending school six days a week, and her family of five was doing well and living together in a two-room home in Port-au-Prince. Although Wadley's house doesn't have a kitchen or a shower and the electricity often doesn't work, she is grateful that there are two large beds, and a table she and her parents and siblings can gather around.

Edwidge Danticat visited Wadley in Haiti a month later. Although Wadley still loved swimming and taking photographs of people, her newest favorite pastime was karate, and she showed off her skills for Edwidge. Wadley was really looking forward to her fourteenth birthday, when she could start taking advanced English classes. As her 2016 school year continued, she studied English intensively on the weekends. Wadley's love of math and science is growing, as is her dream of becoming a doctor.

As all of these girls continue their education, and their ideas and goals expand and evolve, something Edwidge said while being interviewed for the film still resonates:

"People forget that children are children. Little girls are little girls. They play, they dream, they laugh. And they all want the same things. They want a good life, a decent life. . . . They may wear different bows in their hair, some may wear scarves and some may not, but they are still little girls. . . . It certainly makes you want to be a sort of warrior for children who don't have the opportunity to go to school because it's so obvious in their enthusiasm, in their passion, in their dreams, that they all deserve a better future."

Meeting all of these girls who have risen up from their situations and triumphed—as well as learning of the many more who have not yet had that opportunity—has changed me forever. Collectively, these girls have broadened my image of the world, expanded my knowledge, made me angry, made me cry, made me hopeful. It is my sincere wish that meeting them has changed you, too.

Schoolgirls, India.

(Left to right): *Girl Rising* film writer Sooni Taraporevala, Ruksana, *Girl Rising* producer and chief creative officer Martha Adams, and Ruksana's sister Rose.

Room to Read worker Rishi Amatya and *Girl Rising* director Richard Robbins, in Nepal.

Every book poses new challenges, and this book challenged both my writing skills and my sense of who I am as a writer. I have gone on record about the importance of conducting adequate research and doing everything possible to ensure the accuracy of the nonfiction I write, of being transparent when necessary, and of keeping in mind the perspectives of my sources. Of course, I had to do a lot of my own research, but what was different for me in this case was that, for a large percentage of it, I was relying on the research of the *Girl Rising* filmmakers. They were the ones who had traveled the globe and interviewed girls, learning about their backgrounds and inviting them to tell their stories. Girl Rising offered me a treasure trove of research, but the journalist in me also had to learn enough about what their process was in order to understand and trust it.

This entire project was an eye-opening learning experience that broadened my perspective. The things that proved invaluable to me from Girl Rising were (1) the field notes from the director, Richard Robbins, and the producers, and (2) the more than forty-five hours of raw video footage conducted in nine countries with the nine girls who made it into the film, as well as with many other girls who did not. The field notes gave me insights into the emotional aspects of the Western filmmakers—what it was like to be in these far-flung places and begin to grasp what life was like for these girls. The notes were unfiltered impressions, so human, sometimes heartbreaking, sometimes jubilant. I was an armchair traveler, in awe of what they were recording firsthand.

The videos put me right in the room with each girl, allowing me to witness their pains, their joys, their stories. And all of these materials—as any primary sources do—presented nuanced challenges and posed issues for me to ponder. For example, each interview subject told Girl Rising how old she was. What could be simpler—it's a fact delivered directly from the source, right? Except that in many of these countries, documents such as birth certificates are hard to come by or even nonexistent, so a person's birth date is often what a family member recalls and thus is not always accurate. There is no viable way of confirming or denying the information. Likewise, in many poor areas, memorabilia such as photo albums or family scrapbooks or diaries are not commonplace, so again, family anecdotes and memories stem more from oral histories than hard-and-fast records. I had to keep this in mind to piece together the most accurate picture possible.

Girl Rising production manager Alex Dionne, with girls in Ethiopia.

The same can be said, to a certain degree, of the interviews themselves. In each case, I was listening to a girl speak in her native language, and relying on the translator or translators in the room to accurately convey her meaning. In each place, the local translators changed, out of necessity, and with each change came slight differences in approach to translation. That meant that every time I quoted a girl from the video footage I was transcribing, I factored all of that in—taking into account her body language, facial expressions, emotional reactions—all of which helped me gauge whether I felt comfortable enough with a sentence or paragraph to use it. I took the same approach when choosing the images from the thousands of stunning choices Girl Rising provided, which were shot in many different locatons, only using those that had enough identifying information to be compatible with my text.

Another thing I did to check interpretations was to communicate with the film writers. For the film, each of the nine girls was paired with a female writer from that country. Those women got to know the girls face to face, often spending much more time with them off camera, which meant they often had the most insight of anyone on the team. I asked each writer to read my rendition of their girl's story and let me know whether I had captured her properly, and if anything was factually or culturally incorrect.

This was extremely helpful for one other important reason: the film is not a conventional documentary. A few parts of the film were re-created or reimagined by each writer—sometimes in order to protect a girl's identity. If I had questions regarding that, I was able to ask the writer. This is also the reason I did not use any of the screenplay, but started my narrative from scratch. I did not want to risk inadvertently including something from the screenplay that had been fictionalized.

Then there was the unanticipated emotional effect of writing this book. The more I learned, the deeper I wanted to go with the research. Deciding where to stop was difficult. There are more stories out there than dozens of books could ever include. But to be effective with a book like this, one must stay on topic and not overwhelm the reader. And the more stories I discovered, the more devastated I became.

This book nearly wiped me out. But the girls kept me going—their endurance, their stamina, their bravery, their strength. As I went about my daily work, it was from the safety of my warm home, with clean running water and plentiful food, in a country with a free public education system. I had *nothing* to complain about, but I needed

Girl Rising film writer Loung Ung.

psychological breaks from the work. I fell into a rhythm, spending several days immersed in the writing and research, followed by a day off to decompress. It was a gift to have been able to write this book, and I am truly thankful—especially for every girl whose story I was able to listen to and learn from throughout this process. It is quite remarkable that they shared their lives with all of us, and I hope they know what a tremendous impact they have made on the world.

Producer Gina Nemirofsky, with girls in India.

ACKNOWLEDGMENTS

As with every book, there are people without whom the publication process would have been much more difficult, nay, even impossible. They have my deepest gratitude and thanks.

Kayce Freed Jennings, thank you for being at the other end of the phone from that very first day I asked you if writing a Girl Rising book might even be a possibility, and every day after that whenever I needed an ear, a suggestion, a contact, a helping hand. You are a marvel, and I consider myself extremely lucky to have found a new friend in you.

Martha Adams and Sara Hubbard, thank you for your unfailing willingness to answer my questions, share invaluable resources, and puzzle tricky things through. Thank you to the rest of the Girl Rising family, including Tom Yellin, Christina Lowery, Holly Gordon, Colleen Hamilton, Cate Browning, Gina Nemirofsky, Alex Dionne, and Amy Atkinson, who were there whenever I needed to track down or verify information, and the incredible women writers on the film who were kind enough to vet my text about their girls, especially Edwidge Danticat, Maaza Mengiste, Marie Arana, Manjushree Thapa, Loung Ung, Aminatta Forna, and Zarghuna Kargar.

Girl Rising film writer Marie Arana, with Senna.

Richard Robbins, thank you for talking with me, but more importantly, thank you for the astounding work you created with the *Girl Rising* film and for being the human being you are. Martha Adams: that goes for you, too!

Watching the two of you in action (via video footage) and reading your notes from the field brought me to tears more times than I can count.

I would also like to take this opportunity to formally acknowledge the incredible work that Girl Rising has done to support the girls in the film, as well as their families. Of course, each situation is unique, but Girl Rising has worked closely with experienced nonprofit organizations to determine what those needs are and to ensure, as best as possible, that each girl is safe and secure and has the opportunity to complete her education, at least through secondary school. This effort has been supported by Intel Corporation, Girl Rising's founding strategic partner, which has contributed generously to the film and global campaign since the beginning and is committed to supporting the educational needs of the girls and their siblings.

I am extremely grateful for Rosemary Stimola, an agent who is my partner, who is wise and savvy, and who always has my back! Wendy Lamb, thank you for wanting to take the leap and go on this grand adventure with me. Your wisdom always shines through. And to Dana Carey and the team at Wendy Lamb Books/Penguin Random House, especially Angela Carlino, Alison Impey, Heather Kelly, and Stephanie Moss, thank you so much for your talent, passion, and dedication to this project.

Suma (left) with senior producer Kayce Freed Jennings.

Thank you to Eileen Cowell, Laura Ruby, Stephen Kiernan, Dora Sudarsky, Andrea White, Shari Levine, Kristin Johnson Gehsmann, Alison James, Leslie Cahill, and Laurie Stone, who listened while I shared stories, processed how to tell some of them, and were there for quiet time, decompression, and rejuvenating fun.

To Bud (aka D.B.) Stone, thank you for

Girl Rising film writer Maaza Mengiste, with Azmera.

providing the bedrock of my own education, both formal and through infinite daily opportunities for learning since I was small. My foundation for being my own Girl Rising is rooted in your deep love and guidance.

Linda McGinnis, thank you for sharing your infinite wisdom and wealth of knowledge about poverty, women's issues, and the world at large. For taking walks in the woods and being ever ready to engage in deep conversation and challenge the borders of my brain.

Ben Ash, thank you for being generous of mind and spirit, for building fires and lighting candles, and for being an inimitable partner in crime.

Sarah Aronson, your unwavering support, your sisterhood, and your ability to know what I'm trying to say even when I'm failing miserably to say it is astounding. Thank you for being my closest reader, for reminding me of my own process at just the right moments, and for encouraging me to hit the delete button when necessary!

And to my children, Jake and Liza, there are not enough words in the universe to convey my gratitude and love for all the ways you feed my soul. I am truly thankful for this bountiful life we have together. It is a thing of beauty, and I cherish you.

Girl Rising film writer Edwidge Danticat, with Wadley.

Richard Robbins (right), in a Cambodian marketplace.

Girl Rising film writer Aminatta Forna, with Mariama.

BIBLIOGRAPHY

Note: Many of my research materials came from the vast field and primary source research that Girl Rising conducted in making the *Girl Rising* film. All of the primary source footage, interviews, photographs, story archive, and other information they had were made accessible to me for this collaboration. To add more context to all of this information both for readers and myself, I also used the following resources:

BOOKS

Ali, Nujood, with Delphine Minoui. *I Am Nujood, Age 10 and Divorced.* New York: Broadway Books, 2010.

Kargar, Zarghuna. *Dear Zari: The Secret Lives of the Women of Afghanistan.* Naperville, IL: Sourcebooks, 2012.

Kristof, Nicholas D., and Sheryl WuDunn. *Half the Sky: Turning Oppression into Opportunity for Women Worldwide.* New York: Vintage Books/Random House, 2009.

———. *A Path Appears: Transforming Lives, Creating Opportunity.* New York: Knopf, 2014.

Yousafzai, Malala. *I Am Malala: How One Girl Stood Up for Education and Changed the World.* New York: Little Brown, 2014.

ARTICLES

Adams, Martha. "A Vision for Her Village," *USA Today, Media Planet,* October 28, 2011.

Amin, Matiullah, and Shabana Basij-Rasikh. "Empowering Fathers and Daughters," *New York Times International Weekly,* December 16, 2012.

Arana, Marie. "Dreaming of El Dorado," *Virginia Quarterly Review,* Fall 2012, Volume 88, September 17, 2012.

————. "In La Rinconada, Peru, Searching for Beauty in Ugliness," *Washington Post,* March 2, 2013.

Attwood, Karen. "Mona Eltahawy: It's Time to Stop Treating Women Like a Cheap Bargaining Chip," *Independent,* March 8, 2015.

Awake, Mikael. "One Girl's Fight to Learn: An Interview with Writer Maaza Mengiste," *Of Note Magazine,* New York Foundation for the Arts, April 1, 2013.

Bever, Lindsey, and Nick Kirkpatrick. "The Heartbreaking Moment a Kenyan Girl Is Sold into Marriage," *Washington Post,* December 11, 2014.

Bhalla, Nita. "Obama to India: Nations Will Only Succeed If Women Are Successful," Reuters, January 27, 2015.

Brenner, Marie. "The Target," *Vanity Fair,* April 2013.

Brown, Gordon. "Girls Who Risk Their Lives for Education," *New York Times,* April 8, 2013.

Burke, Jason. "Nepal Quake Survivors Face Threat from Human Traffickers Supplying Sex Trade," *Guardian,* May 5, 2015.

Cohen, Elizabeth. "Painful Plight of Haiti's 'Restavec' Children," CNN.com, January 29, 2010.

Conant, Eve. "Afghan Woman Who Once Went to School in Disguise Opens Boarding School for Girls," *National Geographic,* June 21, 2014.

Daragahi, Borzou. "Yemeni Bride, 10, Says I Won't," *Los Angeles Times,* June 11, 2008.

Daugherty, Susan. "A Native Daughter Returns to Afghanistan on Daring Mission: Educating Girls," *National Geographic,* December 11, 2014.

Edwards, Tanya. "The Child Bride Crisis," *Glamour,* July 23, 2014.

Eltahawy, Mona. "Egypt Needs a Revolution Against Sexual Violence," *Guardian,* July 10, 2013.

Gecker, Jocelyn. "Michelle Obama Promoting Girls' Education in Cambodia," Associated Press (via *Huffington Post*), March 20, 2015.

Gladstone, Rick. "Real Threat in a Known Market for Children," *New York Times,* May 7, 2014.

Gorney, Cynthia. "Too Young to Wed," *National Geographic,* June 2011.

Hanson, Jody. "Get Inspired by Sokha Chen," *Audrey Magazine,* Fall 2014.

Hauser, Christine. "Yemen Takes a Step Toward Law Ending Child Marriage," *New York Times,* January 23, 2014.

Hile, Jennifer. "In Cambodia's Biggest Dump, School Offers Hope," *National Geographic Today,* September 12, 2003.

Johnson, K.C. "The Big Picture," *Chicago Tribune,* December 24, 2006.

————. "Dream Catchers: A New Day, New Lives," *Chicago Tribune,* December 24, 2007.

Kannampilly, Ammu. "No Justice for Nepal's Slave Girls," *The Star Online,* February 9, 2014.

Kristof, Nicholas. "A Girl's Escape," *New York Times,* January 1, 2014.

————. "Divorced Before Puberty," *New York Times,* March 4, 2010.

————. "We Start a School in Cambodia," *New York Times,* December 29, 2008.

Lacey, Marc. "Children in Servitude, the Poorest of Haiti's Poor," *New York Times,* September 14, 2008.

Levine, Samantha. "Two Girls Rising," *Daily Beast,* April 4, 2014.

Loney, Jim. "Haiti 'Restavek' Tradition Called Child Slavery," Reuters, February 18, 2010.

Machel, Graça, and Desmond Tutu. "Child Marriage Robs Girls of Their Opportunities," *Washington Post,* July 30, 2012.

Machel, Graça, Emilia Pires, and Gunilla Carlsson. "The World We Want: An End to Child Marriage," *Lancet,* September 21, 2013.

MacKenzie, Jean. "An Afghan Woman's Journey from 'Secret School' to Mentoring a Generation of Girls," Public Radio International (PRI), The GroundTruth Project, April 22, 2015.

Maseko, Nomsa. "Tutu and Machel Speak Out Against Child Marriage," *BBC News Africa,* July 1, 2014.

———. "Zambian Child Bride: 'I Was Forced to Marry a Stranger,'" *BBC News Africa,* July 22, 2014.

Mensch, Barbara S., Susheela Singh, and John B. Casterline. "Trends in the Timing of First Marriage Among Men and Women in the Developing World," in Cynthia B. Lloyd, Jere R. Behrman, Nelly P. Stromquist, and Barney Cohen (eds.), *The Changing Transitions to Adulthood in Developing Countries: Selected Studies* (pp. 118–171), Washington, DC: National Academies Press, 2005.

Newton, Paula. "Child Bride's Nightmare After Divorce," CNN.com, August 28, 2009.

"No Ceilings: The Full Participation Report," Research & Analysis by the Economist Intelligence Unit and the WORLD Policy Analysis Center, March 2015.

Obama, Michelle. "The First Lady's Travel Journal: Educating and Empowering Girls in Cambodia," The White House Blog, March 21, 2015.

"PM Modi Launches Sukanya Samridhi Yojna Under Beti Bachao Campaign," Press Trust of India, January 22, 2015.

Power, Carla. "Nujood Ali & Shada Nasser: The Voices for Children," *Glamour,* November 2008.

Qureshi, Huma. "Zarghuna Kargar on Taking Part in *Girl Rising*," *National,* March 7, 2013.

Raghavan, Sudarsan. "In Niger, Hunger Crisis Raises Fears of More Child Marriages," *Washington Post,* July 9, 2012.

Robbins, Richard E. "Women in the World: Sokha Chen, Cambodia," *Daily Beast,* March 6, 2011.

Robertson, Nic. "Shelter Tries to Help Abused Child Brides," CNN.com, June 10, 2010.

Rubin, Alissa J. "Rebelling Against Abuse, Afghan Women See Signs of Change," *New York Times,* May 27, 2014.

"Saudi Child 'Files for Divorce,'" *BBC News,* August 24, 2008.

"Saudis 'to Regulate' Child Brides," *BBC News,* April 15, 2009.

Sharma, Kalpana. "The Other Half: We Should Be Ashamed," *Hindu,* January 21, 2012.

Sheffer, Joe. "Yemen's Youngest Divorcee Says Father Has Squandered Cash from Her Book," *Guardian,* March 12, 2013.

Smith, Lydia. "International Day for the Abolition of Slavery: Why We Need to End Child Marriage," *International Business Times,* December 2, 2014.

Sweis, Rana F. "In Jordan, Ever Younger Syrian Brides," *New York Times,* September 14, 2013.

Tutu, Desmond. "A Message to Men and Boys About Child Marriage," TheElders.org, September 20, 2011.

"U.S. Secretary of Education Arne Duncan Meets 'Girl Rising' Star in Haiti," PartnersinHealth.org, November 7, 2013.

Worth, Robert F. "Tiny Voices Defy Child Marriage in Yemen," *New York Times,* June 29, 2008.

"Young Saudi Girl's Marriage Ended," *BBC News,* April 30, 2009.

REPORTS

Atkinson, Amy. Afghanistan Trip Diary, October 2011.

"A Way to Go: An Update on Implementation of the Law on Elimination of Violence Against Women in Afghanistan," Created by the United Nations Assistance Mission in Afghanistan and United Nations Office of the High Commissioner for Human Rights. Kabul, Afghanistan, December 2013.

"Background Paper on Attacks Against Girls Seeking to Access Education," United Nations Human Rights Report, February 2015, ohchr.org/Documents/HRBodies/CEDAW/Report_attacks_on_girls_Feb2015.pdf.

"Cash Transfer Programs for Gender Equality in Girls' Secondary Education," United Nations Girls' Education Initiative (UNGEI) and Global Partnership for Education, April 2014.

Chaaban, Jad, and Wendy Cunningham. "Measuring the Economic Gain of Investing in Girls: The Girl Effect Dividend," The World Bank Human Development Network Children and Youth Unit & Poverty Reduction and Economic Management Network, Gender Unit, August 2011, http://www-wds.worldbank.org/external/default/WDSContentServer/WDSP/IB/2011/08/08/000158349_20110808092702/Rendered/PDF/WPS5753.pdf.

"Girl Rising/Global Fund for Women Progress Report: Transforming Education for Girls in Haiti," Partners in Health, May 2015.

"Global Report on Trafficking in Persons, 2014," Created by the United Nations Office on Drugs and Crime (UNODC) United Nations publication, Sales No. E.14.V.10, unodc.org/documents/data-and-analysis/glotip/GLOTIP_2014_full_report.pdf.

Harper, Caroline, Nicola Jones, Elizabeth Presler-Marshall, and David Walker. "Unhappily Ever After: Slow and Uneven Progress in the Fight Against Early Marriage," Overseas Development Institute, London, July 2014.

"Make It Right: Ending the Crises in Girls' Education," A Report by the Global Campaign for Education & RESULTS Educational Fund, ungei.org/resources/files/MakeItRight_Report_07.pdf.

"Marrying Too Young: End Child Marriage," United Nations Population Fund, New York, New York, 2012, unfpa.org/sites/default/files/pub-pdf/MarryingTooYoung.pdf.

Murphy, Shannon, with Wivinia Belmonte and Jane Nelson. "Investing in Girls' Education: An Opportunity for Corporate Leadership," Corporate Social Responsibility Initiative, Harvard Kennedy School, September 2009, hks.harvard.edu/mrcbg/CSRI/publications/report_40_investing_in_girls.pdf.

"No Place for Children: Child Recruitment, Forced Marriage, and Attacks on Schools in Somalia," Human Rights Watch, February 20, 2012, hrw.org/sites/default/files/reports/somalia0212ForUpload_0.pdf.

Reissman, Hailey. "Spotlight TEDx Talk: Can a Comic Book Overcome India's Menstruation Taboo?" TEDx Innovations, November 19, 2014.

"Restavèk: The Persistence of Child Labor and Slavery," Submission to the United Nations Universal Periodic Review, Twelfth Session of the Working Group on the UPR Human Rights Council, October 3–14, 2011. Submitted by Restavèk Freedom.

Robbins, Richard, and Martha Adams. "Notes from the Field," December 11, 2010–March 1, 2012.

"State of the World's Children 2015: Reimagine the Future: Innovation for Every Child." United Nation's Children's Fund, November 2014.

"Voice and Agency: Empowering Women and Girls for Shared Prosperity," The World Bank, 2014.

VIDEOS

Chen, Sokha. "My Bittersweet Life Story," Digital Storytelling Contest (DISTCO), April 7, 2014, youtube.com/watch?v=m_kqtib-6iw.

CNN, March 21, 2014, "From Child of Dump to Star Student," youtube.com/watch?v=mZktn68TX3k.

Ellick, Adam B. "A Schoolgirl's Odyssey," *New York Times,* October 10, 2009.

Girl Rising, short video update on Senna, April 15, 2014, youtube.com/watch?v=N_HgVMyaBO8.

Hannah Godefa, Interview by Tefera Gedamu on Ethiopian TV, published September 10, 2012, youtube.com/watch?v=OqCTZM_nTaU.

London, Jennifer. "Book Publishing Program Helps One Young Author in Nepal Find Her Voice (and Her Way Back to School)," Reel News Productions, for Room to Read, September 19, 2012.

Newton, Paula. "World's Untold Stories: Wedlocked," CNN.com, August 28, 2009.

No Ceilings, 2015. "Not There Yet: A Data Driven Analysis of Gender Equality," March 9, 2015, Shabana Basij-Rasikh and Uzma, livestream.com/accounts/4884897/events/3867842.

Shabana Basij-Rasikh Speaks on International Day of the Girl | 10x10, October 2012, vimeo.com/53020620.

"Shabana Basij-Rasikh: Dare to Educate Afghan Girls," TedxWomen 2012, filmed December 2012, ted.com/talks/shabana_basij_rasikh_dare_to_educate_afghan_girls?language=en#t-369642.

Tall as the Boabab Tree, Sundance Artist Services and the San Francisco Film Society, tallasthebaobabtree.com/watch/.

TEDxBangalore Aditi Gupta, *Menstrupedia,* November 19, 2014, tedxinnovations.ted.com/2014/11/19/tedx-talk-spotlight-can-a-comic-book-overcome-indias-menstruation-taboo/.

WEBSITES

Afghan Women's Writing Project: awwproject.org
A New Day Cambodia: anewdaycambodia.com
The CNN Freedom Project: thecnnfreedomproject.blogs.cnn.com
The Elders: theelders.org
Fair Trade USA: fairtradeusa.org
Free the Slaves: freetheslaves.net
Girl Rising: girlrising.com
Girl Up: girlup.org
Hannah Godefa and Pencil Mountain: hannahgodefa.com
Nepal Youth Foundation: nepalyouthfoundation.org
Prerana: preranaantitrafficking.org
Restavèk Freedom: restavekfreedom.org
Room to Read: roomtoread.org
United Nations Human Rights: un.org/en/rights
United Nations Office on Drugs and Crime: unodc.org
Wheels 4 Life: wheels4life.org
World Bicycle Relief: worldbicyclerelief.org

SOURCE NOTES

All source references are cited in full in bibliography.

Part One

p. 2: "My life would mean . . ." Douaa, Girl Rising Story Archive.

p. 2: "Life without an education . . ." Purnima, Girl Rising Story Archive.

p. 2: "When you get an education . . ." Priya ,Girl Rising Story Archive.

p. 4: "I want to stand for . . ." Fanta, Girl Rising Story Archive.

p. 5: ". . . there are a million young Malalas." Brown, "Girls Who Risk Their Lives for Education."

p. 6: "I want to share my . . ." Rosemarrie, Girl Rising Story Archive.

p. 7: "When a girl goes to school . . ." Bhalla, "Obama to India: Nations Will Only Succeed If Women Are Successful."

Part Two

p. 17: "When I saw other children . . ." Adams, "Notes from the Field."

p. 19: "My family needed me to work . . ." Douaa, Girl Rising Story Archive.

Modern-Day Slavery

p. 22: "I feel strong when . . ." Marilu, Girl Rising Story Archive.

p. 23: "There has never been . . ." Gladstone, "Real Threat in a Known Market for Children."

p. 25: "funny and animated" and "lights up the room." Adams, "Notes from the Field."

p. 27: "Many of them are treated . . ." Lacey, "Children in Servitude, the Poorest of Haiti's Poor."

p. 29: "The parents aren't bad . . ." Cohen, "Painful Plight of Haiti's 'Restavec' Children."

p. 32: "I was so scared . . ." Kannampilly, "No Justice for Nepal's Slave Girls."

p. 35: "It's pretty hard . . ." Robbins, "Notes from the Field."

p. 36: "And so this girl . . ." Robbins, "Notes from the Field."

p. 41: "It's similar to when you . . ." Suma, *Girl Rising* interview footage.

p. 41: "They made me sleep . . ." Suma, speaking to Manjushree Thapa for Girl Rising.

p. 41: "I felt as though . . ." Suma, *Girl Rising* interview footage.

p. 42: "What tends to happen . . ." Suma, *Girl Rising* interview footage.

p. 42: "One day, a social worker . . ." Suma, speaking to Manjushree Thapa for Girl Rising.

p. 43: "I wanted to fight . . ." Suma, speaking to Manjushree Thapa for Girl Rising.

p. 44: "I love all my teachers . . ." Suma, *Girl Rising* interview footage.

p. 44: "Education is like the light . . ." Suma, *Girl Rising* interview footage.

p. 44: "Even though the government . . ." Suma, *Girl Rising* interview footage.

p. 44: "I want to work . . ." Suma, *Girl Rising* interview footage.

p. 44: "The girls talked about . . ." Robbins, "Notes from the Field."

p. 45: "As far back as I can remember . . ." Suma, *Girl Rising* interview footage.

p. 45: "In this [second] house . . ." and "learned how to sing . . ." Suma, speaking to Manjushree Thapa, for Girl Rising.

p. 45: "I wrote that song . . ." Suma, *Girl Rising* interview footage.

Child Marriage

p. 49: "In developing nations . . ." World Health Organization. "Adolescent Pregnancy." http://www.who.int/mediacentre/factsheets/fs364/en/index.html.

p. 54: "was no longer their responsibility . . ." and "My husband won't allow . . ." Maseko, "Zambian Child Bride: 'I was forced to marry a stranger.'"

p. 56: "The fear is, if the food crisis . . ." Raghavan, "In Niger, Hunger Crisis Raises Fears of More Child Marriages."

p. 56: "These families feel marriage . . ." Sweis, "In Jordan, Ever Younger Syrian Brides."

p. 57: "The outsider's impulse . . ." Gorney, "Too Young to Wed."

p. 57: "Parents feel like they have to . . ." Maaza Mengiste, *Girl Rising* interview footage.

p. 63: "Afghanistan went through . . ." and "During that time . . ." Zarghuna Kargar, *Girl Rising* interview footage.

p. 64: "I note the rage . . ." and "She proudly blinks back . . ." Atkinson, Afghanistan Trip Diary.

p. 65: "He will kill me." Atkinson, Afghanistan Trip Diary.

p. 65: "She had that passion . . ." Zarghuna Kargar, *Girl Rising* interview footage.

p. 69: "I'm going to open my heart . . ." Mona Eltahawy, *Girl Rising* interview footage.

p. 69: "rarely, if ever . . ." Eltahawy, "Egypt Needs a Revolution Against Sexual Violence."

p. 69: "I know where she got . . ." Mona Eltahawy, *Girl Rising* interview footage.

p. 70: "I came to get . . ." Daragahi, "Yemeni Bride, 10, Says I Won't."

p. 70: "When I married . . ." Newton, "World's Untold Stories: Wedlocked."

p. 70: "When she told me . . ." Newton, "World's Untold Stories: Wedlocked."

p. 70: "All women must . . ." Ali, Nujood, with Delphine Minoui, p. 96.

p. 71: "I'm a simple village . . ." Ali, Nujood, with Delphine Minoui, p. 18.

p. 71: "No one has ever . . ." Ali, Nujood, with Delphine Minoui, p. 79.

p. 72: "I did it so that people . . ." Newton, "World's Untold Stories: Wedlocked."

p. 72: "We were lucky . . ." Worth, "Tiny Voices Defy Child Marriage in Yemen."

p. 72: "Seven months ago, I . . ." Newton, "World's Untold Stories: Wedlocked."

p. 72: "There's no change . . ." Newton, "World's Untold Stories: Wedlocked."

p. 72: "I've been asked to leave . . ." Sheffer, "Yemen's Youngest Divorcee Says Father Has Squandered Cash from Her Book."

p. 73: "Her case was . . ." Gorney, "Too Young to Wed."

p. 73: "If there were any danger . . ." Gorney, "Too Young to Wed."

p. 75: "I was fourteen. I had . . ." Melka, *Girl Rising* interview footage.

p. 75: "I didn't want to . . ." Melka, *Girl Rising* interview footage.

p. 75–76: "When my parents got out . . ." and "It was hard, but . . ." Melka, *Girl Rising* interview footage.

p. 77: "Recess" and "A doctor" and "Ethiopia is economically . . ." Aseya, *Girl Rising* interview footage.

p. 77: "I'm going to be married . . ." and "Then I will leave . . ." Aseya, *Girl Rising* interview footage.

p. 78: "You are knocking down . . ." Banchiayehu, *Girl Rising* interview footage.

p. 79: "They are proud . . ." Banchiayehu, *Girl Rising* interview footage.

p. 81: "They do not smile easily . . ." Robbins, "Notes from the Field."

p. 82: "Each of our stories pivots . . ." Maaza Mengiste, *Girl Rising* film.

p. 83: "I got mad and . . ." Azmera, *Girl Rising* interview footage.

p. 84: "It's not only in what you can . . ." Maseko, "Tutu and Machel Speak Out Against Child Marriage."

p. 84: "My hope for Azmera . . ." Maaza Mengiste, *Girl Rising* interview footage.

p. 85: "I want to be an author . . ." and "Because of our financial . . ." and "I have seen their sufferings . . ." and "We will do whatever we can . . ." London, "Book Publishing Program Helps One Young Author in Nepal Find Her Voice (and Her Way Back to School)."

Limited Access—or None at All

p. 87: "A girl on planet Earth . . . into poverty." Martin Ravalion and Shaohua Chen. "The developing world is poorer than we thought but no less successful in the fight against poverty." The World Bank. August 2008. https://openknowledge.worldbank.org/bitstream/handle/10986/6322/WPS4703.pdf?sequence=1.

p. 87: "School is not free . . . 50 countries." UNESCO. Global Monitoring Report, 2011. http://unesdoc.unesco.org/images/0019/001907/190743e.pdf.

p. 89: "What is the point . . ." Sharma, "The Other Half: We Should Be Ashamed."

p. 93: "She doesn't understand . . ." Adams, "Notes from the Field."

p. 95: "beamed with pride . . ." Adams, "Notes from the Field."

p. 95: "a fire inside her" and "When I see my teacher . . ." Adams, "Notes from the Field."

p. 96: "Attacks against girls . . ." "Background Paper on Attacks Against Girls Seeking to Access Education," United Nations Human Rights Report.

p. 97: "An educated person . . ." Nazma, Girl Rising Story Archive.

p. 100: "In Haiti, something like . . ." Edwidge Danticat, *Girl Rising* interview footage.

p. 100: "Wandering through a tent camp . . ." Robbins, "Notes from the Field."

p. 101: "She, for me, embodies the hope . . ." Edwidge Danticat, *Girl Rising* interview footage.

p. 105: "I had no choice . . ." "From Child of Dump to Star Student," CNN.

p. 105: "I always thought my life . . ." Chen, "My Bittersweet Life Story."

p. 105: "When I first arrived . . ." Sokha, *Girl Rising* interview footage.

p. 105: "I love reading." Sokha, *Girl Rising* interview footage.

p. 106: "When I was young . . ." Sokha, *Girl Rising* interview footage.

p. 107: "nerves of steel . . ." Loung Ung, *Girl Rising* interview footage.

p. 107: "I see the little girls . . ." and "What do you think . . ." and "Maybe they think . . ." Sokha & Loung Ung, *Girl Rising* interview footage.

p. 107: "Over the time we . . ." Robbins, "Notes from the Field."

p. 108: "I want to be . . ." Sokha & Loung Ung, *Girl Rising* interview footage.

p. 112: "The scrub is gone . . ." Arana, "Dreaming of El Dorado."

p. 114: "He used to give us . . ." Senna, *Girl Rising* interview footage.

p. 114: "The life of a child . . ." Senna, *Girl Rising* interview footage.

p. 115: "In the middle of a conversation . . ." Marie Arana, *Girl Rising* interview footage.

p. 115: "I would concentrate on . . ." and "I see myself . . ." Senna, *Girl Rising* interview footage.

p. 116: "Yes, I will be back . . ." Senna, *Girl Rising* interview footage.

p. 116: "I think you can . . ." Senna, *Girl Rising* interview footage.

p. 116: "What struck me most . . ." Marie Arana and Senna, *Girl Rising* interview footage.

p. 116: "From my family . . ." and "going to triumph . . ." Senna, *Girl Rising* interview footage.

p. 118: "I don't think, that first . . ." Senna, *Girl Rising* interview footage.

p. 118: "It's a way to reflect . . ." and "My heart." Senna, *Girl Rising* interview footage.

p. 121: "They live on the pavement . . ." Sooni Taraporevala, *Girl Rising* interview footage.

p. 121: "Water is a good walk . . ." Adams, "Notes from the Field."

p. 122: "Hand in hand, Ruskana . . ." Adams, "Notes from the Field."

p. 122: "Arriving at Ruksana's tarp . . ." Adams, "Notes from the Field."

p. 122: "but only if the film . . ." Adams, "Notes from the Field."

p. 124: "She is doing so well . . ." Sooni Taraporevala, *Girl Rising* interview footage.

p. 127: "The Sierra Leone of my childhood . . ." Aminatta Forna, *Girl Rising* interview footage.

p. 127: "Now I'm seeing the restoration . . ." Aminatta Forna, *Girl Rising* interview footage.

p. 128: "Mariama is so much like . . ." Aminatta Forna, *Girl Rising* interview footage.

p. 128: "We were at the school . . ." Aminatta Forna, *Girl Rising* interview footage.

p. 128: "In the postwar years . . ." Aminatta Forna, *Girl Rising* interview footage.

p. 129: "It's something that she obviously loves . . ." Aminatta Forna, *Girl Rising* interview footage.

p. 129: "I was so, so shy . . ." Mariama, *Girl Rising* interview footage.

p. 131: "At first, when a child wants . . ." M'ballu, *Girl Rising* interview footage.

p. 131: "The little that she has . . ." M'ballu, *Girl Rising* interview footage.

p. 131: "When I go on the radio . . ." M'ballu, *Girl Rising* interview footage.

p. 131: "If I go to school . . ." M'ballu, *Girl Rising* interview footage.

p. 131: "My daughter will have to . . ." M'ballu, *Girl Rising* interview footage.

p. 133: "Most of my lifetime . . ." Pricilla, *Girl Rising* interview footage.

p. 133: "they abandoned me because . . ." Pricilla, *Girl Rising* interview footage.

p. 133: "I like to serve the ball . . ." Pricilla, *Girl Rising* interview footage.

p. 133: "I like that book . . ." Pricilla, *Girl Rising* interview footage.

p. 133: "I wish that when I am educated . . ." Pricilla, *Girl Rising* interview footage.

p. 133: "I want him to strengthen education . . ." Pricilla, *Girl Rising* interview footage.

p. 133: "We all are the same . . ." Pricilla, *Girl Rising* interview footage.

p. 134: "You can lose everything . . ." "Shabana Basij-Rasikh: Dare to Educate Afghan Girls."

p. 134: "Behind every successful woman . . ." Shabana Basij-Rasikh Speaks on International Day of the Girl.

p. 134: "My effort to educate . . ." and "If my father can stand up . . ." Amin, Matiullah, and Shabana Basij-Rasikh, "Empowering Fathers and Daughters."

p. 134: "My parents are my role models . . ." Amin, Matiullah, and Shabana Basij-Rasikh, "Not There Yet: A Data Driven Analysis of Gender Equality."

p. 135: "I think we are always . . ." Robbins, "Notes from the Field."

Part Three

p. 138: "You don't have to be thirty . . ." hannahgodefa.com.

p. 139: "You can go to a *real* school . . ." Shabana Basij-Rasikh Speaks on International Day of the Girl.

p. 140: "People usually appreciate . . ." MacKenzie, "An Afghan Woman's Journey from 'Secret School' to Mentoring a Generation of Girls."

p. 146: "Child marriage occurs . . ." and "I want to encourage boys . . ." Tutu, "A Message to Men and Boys About Child Marriage."

p. 148: "I really had a vision . . ." Hannah Godefah interview by Tefera Gedamu on Ethiopian TV. youtube.com/watch?v=OqCTZM_nTaU.

p. 148: "At first, he really didn't . . ." Hannah Godefah interview by Tefera Gedamu on Ethiopian TV. youtube.com/watch?v=OqCTZM_nTaU.

p. 148: "I have a social responsibility . . ." Hannah Godefah interview by Tefera Gedamu on Ethiopian TV. youtube.com/watch?v=OqCTZM_nTaU.

p. 152: "That was awesome . . ." and "The languages were Wolof . . ." Private correspondence between Sokha and Tanya Lee Stone.

p. 153: "It was wonderful . . ." and "I love reading books . . ." Private correspondence between Sokha and Tanya Lee Stone.

p. 154: "My life has changed . . ." *Girl Rising* short video update on Senna, April 15, 2014. youtube.com/watch?v=N_HgVMyaBO8.

p. 154: "I feel happy about . . ." *Girl Rising* short video update on Senna, April 15, 2014. youtube.com/watch?v=N_HgVMyaBO8.

p. 155: "I think it's not going to be easy . . ." Senna, *Girl Rising* interview footage.

p. 156: "No one asked me . . ." Melka, *Girl Rising* interview footage.

p. 157: "It was really sweet . . ." "U.S. Secretary of Education Arne Duncan Meets '*Girl Rising*' Star in Haiti."

p. 158: "People forget that children . . ." Edwidge Danticat, *Girl Rising* interview footage.

Richard Robbins and Gina Nemirofsky (behind camera), in Haiti.

PHOTOGRAPH CREDITS

p. vi: Anindan Choudhury, courtesy of Girl Rising.

p. vii: Gina Nemirofsky, courtesy of Girl Rising.

p. 1: Martha Adams, Richard E. Robbins, Gina Nemirofsky; courtesy of Girl Rising.

pp. 2, 4: Gina Nemirofsky, courtesy of Girl Rising.

p. 6: Martha Adams, courtesy of Girl Rising.

p. 10: (Jamileth) Martha Adams.

p. 11: (Neelam) Martha Adams and Gina Nemirofsky. (Nerlande, Sita) Martha Adams. (Sarah) Gina Nemirofsky. All courtesy of Girl Rising.

p. 12: (Nazma) Martha Adams and Gina Nemirofsky, courtesy of Girl Rising. (Lydia, Clarita, Pricilla) Gina Nemirofsky. (Wendjie) Martha Adams. (Hoda) Jenna Millman. All courtesy of Girl Rising.

p. 13: (Asha, Sopatt, Soltha, Ruksana) Martha Adams. (Azmera) Alex Dionne. (Wadley) John Valme. (Senna, Mariama, M'Ballu) Gina Nemirofsky. (Suma) Rishi Amataya. (Banchiayehu) Richard E. Robbins and Alex Dionne. (Yasmin) All courtesy of Girl Rising.

p. 14–15: Martha Adams, courtesy of Girl Rising.

p. 16: Richard E. Robbins and Alex Dionne, courtesy of Girl Rising.

pp. 17, 19: Gina Nemirofsky, courtesy of Girl Rising.

pp. 20–21: Anindan Choudhury, courtesy of Girl Rising.

p. 22: Gina Nemirofsky, courtesy of Girl Rising.

p. 24: Martha Adams and Gina Nemirofsky, courtesy of Girl Rising.

p. 26: Martha Adams, courtesy of Girl Rising.

pp. 28–29: John Valme, courtesy of Girl Rising.

p. 30: Anindan Choudhury, courtesy of Girl Rising.

p. 33: Martha Adams, courtesy of Girl Rising.

pp. 34, 37: Gina Nemirofsky, courtesy of Girl Rising.

pp. 38, 40: Martha Adams, courtesy of Girl Rising.

p. 43: Anindan Choudhury, courtesy of Girl Rising.

pp. 45, 46–47: Alex Dionne, courtesy of Girl Rising.

pp. 48–49: Richard E. Robbins and Alex Dionne, courtesy of Girl Rising.

p. 52: Nicole Whitaker, courtesy of Girl Rising.

pp. 58, 60, 62, 64, 66: courtesy of Girl Rising.

p. 68: Oliver Wilkins, courtesy of Girl Rising.

p. 74: Richard E. Robbins and Alex Dionne, courtesy of Girl Rising.

p. 76: courtesy of Girl Rising.

p. 79: courtesy of Girl Rising.

p. 80: Nicole Whitaker, courtesy of Girl Rising.

p. 82: Alex Dionne, courtesy of Girl Rising.

p. 85: Gina Nemirofsky, courtesy of Girl Rising.

pp. 86–87: Martha Adams, courtesy of Girl Rising.

p. 88: Richard E. Robbins and Alex Dionne, courtesy of Girl Rising.

pp. 90–91, 92, 93, 94: Martha Adams, courtesy of Girl Rising.

p. 97: Rajarshi Sengupta, courtesy of Girl Rising.

pp. 98, 101: John Valme, courtesy of Girl Rising.

pp. 102, 103, 106, 108, 109: Martha Adams, courtesy of Girl Rising.

p. 110: courtesy of Girl Rising.

p. 111: Edgar Jiron, courtesy of Girl Rising.

p. 113: Jose Madalengoitia, courtesy of Girl Rising.

p. 117: Gina Nemirofsky, courtesy of Girl Rising.

p. 118: courtesy of Girl Rising.

pp. 120, 123: Martha Adams and Gina Nemirofsky, courtesy of Girl Rising.

pp. 124, 125: Martha Adams, courtesy of Girl Rising.

pp. 126, 129, 130, 132: Gina Nemirofsky, courtesy of Girl Rising.

p. 134: courtesy of Lalage Snow.

p. 135: courtesy of Girl Rising.

pp. 136–137: Gina Nemirofsky, courtesy of Girl Rising.

p. 138: ©UNICEF Ethiopia/2012/Dixon.

p. 140: Kayce Freed Jennings, courtesy of Girl Rising.

p. 142: courtesy of Aditi Gupta/Menstrupedia

p. 145: Martha Adams, courtesy of Girl Rising.

p. 146: public domain photo by Benny Gool.

p. 149: ©UNICEF Ethiopia/2012/Dixon.

pp. 150–151, 152: courtesy of Girl Rising.

p. 153: Gina Nemirofsky, courtesy of Girl Rising.

p. 154: (Suma) Rishi Govinda Amatya, courtesy of Girl Rising.

p. 154: (Senna) Francisco Levi/CARE.

p. 155: (Mariama) Michael Kamara.

p. 156: (Ruksana) Tess Joseph. (Melka) Alex Dionne. Both courtesy of Girl Rising.

p. 157: (Azmera) courtesy of World Vision.

p. 157: (Wadley) John Valme, courtesy of Girl Rising.

p. 159: Martha Adams and Gina Nemirofsky, courtesy of Girl Rising.

p. 160: (top) Gina Nemirofsky, courtesy of Girl Rising. (bottom) Martha Adams, courtesy of Girl Rising.

p. 162: Justin Reeves, courtesy of Girl Rising.

p. 163: Martha Adams, courtesy of Girl Rising.

p. 164: Martha Adams, courtesy of Girl Rising.

p. 165: Gina Nemirofsky, courtesy of Girl Rising

p. 166: Alex Dionne, courtesy of Girl Rising.

p. 167: (top) Alex Dionne, courtesy of Girl Rising. (bottom) John Valme, courtesy of Girl Rising.

p. 168: (top) Martha Adams, courtesy of Girl Rising. (bottom) Gina Nemirofsky, courtesy of Girl Rising.

p. 180: Martha Adams, courtesy of Girl Rising.

p. 182: Martha Adams, courtesy of Girl Rising.

p. 192: courtesy of Ashlee Nalette.

Richard Robbins, in Cambodia.

Nonprofit and Nongovernmental Organizations

The organizations listed are either mentioned in this book or were an inspiration to the Girl Rising team during research and filming trips for the *Girl Rising* movie.

Afghan Women's Writing Project
Asociación Huarayo (The Huarayo Association)
A New Day Cambodia
Cambodia's Children Education Fund
CARE
Centre of Action and Development (CAD)
The Elders
Friends of Needy Children (FNC)
Girl Up (a United Nations program)
Girls Not Brides
The Harpswell Foundation
Hope Village Society (HVS)
Magic Bus USA
Nepal Youth Foundation (NYF)
Partners in Health (PIH)
People Improvement Organization (PIO)
Pink Bike
Plan International
Prerana
Restavèk Freedom

Room to Read
School of Leadership Afghanistan (SOLA)
UNICEF
Wheels 4 Life
World Bicycle Relief
World Vision

Rates of Child Marriage Around the World

This is additional information for the map on pages 50–51.

Countries with less than 2% or no data available:
Andorra, Angola, Antigua and Barbuda, Argentina, Australia, Austria, Bahamas, Bahrain, Barbados, Belgium, Botswana, Brunei Darussalam, Bulgaria, Canada, Chile, China, Cook Islands, Croatia, Cyprus, Czech Republic, Democratic People's Republic of Korea, Denmark, Dominica, Estonia, Fiji, Finland, Germany, Greece, Granada, Holy See, Hungary, Iceland, Ireland, Israel, Italy, Japan, Kuwait, Latvia, Libya, Liechtenstein, Lithuania, Luxembourg, Malaysia, Malta, Mauritius, Micronesia, Monaco, Myanmar, Netherlands, New Zealand, Niue, Norway, Oman, Palau, Panama, Poland, Portugal, Qatar, Republic of Korea, Romania, Russian Federation, Saint Kitts and Nevis, Saint Vincent and Grenadines, Samoa, San Marino, Saudi Arabia, Seychelles, Singapore, Slovakia, Slovenia, Spain, Sweden, Switzerland, Turkmenistan, United Arab Emirates, United Kingdom, United States, Uruguay, Venezuela

INDEX

Note: *Italic* page numbers refer to illustrations.

Tanya Lee Stone.

ABOUT THE AUTHOR

Tanya Lee Stone has received many awards and honors for her books, including an NAACP Image Award for *Courage Has No Color,* a Robert F. Sibert Medal for *Almost Astronauts,* and a Golden Kite Award for *The Good, the Bad, and the Barbie.* Her articles and reviews have appeared in *School Library Journal,* the *Horn Book Magazine,* and the *New York Times.* She is noted for her passion for telling little-known or unknown true stories of people who have been missing from our histories. Stone went to Oberlin College and now teaches writing at Champlain College. You can find her online at tanyastone.com, on facebook.com/tanyastone, and on Twitter at @TanyaLeeStone.